THE BEST OF AMSTERDAM IN 6 WALKS

MOON AMSTERDAM WALKS

Step off the plane and head to the newest, hippest café in town. Find out where to get the best fish in the city or where there is locally brewed beer on tap. In *Moon Amsterdam Walks*, you'll find inside information on numerous hidden gems. Skip the busy shopping streets and stroll through the city at your own pace, taking in a local attraction on your way to the latest and greatest concept stores. Savor every second and make your trip a truly great experience.

AMSTERDAM-BOUND!

Amsterdam is a compact city and a multicultural melting pot with open-minded inhabitants. There's a reason people say anything goes in Amsterdam. What makes Amsterdam so special are its numerous, splendid museums and the incredibly diverse range of shops—from vintage and design to trendy pop-up stores—all to be found in central neighborhoods, together with the most varied restaurants, new eateries, and pubs. The suburbs also provide a raw industrial feel with numerous festivals, underground parties, and secondhand markets. We'll take you to Amsterdam's most fascinating places.

ABOUT THIS BOOK

In this book, you'll discover the genuine highlights of the city we love. Discover the city by foot and at your own pace, so you can relax and experience the local lifestyle without having to prepare a lot beforehand. That means more time for you. These walks take you past our favorite restaurants, cafés, museums, galleries, shops, and other notable attractions—places locals like to go to. So who knows, you might even run into us.

None of the places mentioned here has paid to appear in either the text or the photos, and all text has been written by an independent editorial staff.

<u>CITY</u>
AMSTERDAM

<u>WORK & ACTIVITIES</u>
**PHOTOGRAPHER
AND BLOGGER**

<u>LOCAL</u>
FEMKE DAM

Femke knows the city better than many of its natives and likes nothing more than sharing her love of Amsterdam. She especially enjoys discovering new cafés, picnicking in Westerpark, and relaxing on Sunday evenings when Amsterdam has that village feel. A personal favorite of hers: taking the ferry to Amsterdam-Noord—it's almost like going on vacation.

PRACTICAL INFORMATION

The six walks in this book allow you to discover the best neighborhoods in the city by foot at your own pace. The walks will lead you to museums and notable attractions; more importantly they'll show you where to go for good food, drinks, shopping, entertainment, and an overall good time. Check out the map at the front of this book to see the areas of the city where the walks will take you.

Each route is clearly indicated on a detailed map at the beginning of the relevant chapter. The map also specifies where each place is located. The color of the number tells you what type of venue it is (see legend the at the bottom of this page). A description of each place is given later in the chapter.

Without taking into consideration extended stops at various locations, each walk should take a maximum of three hours. The approximate distance is indicated at the top of the page before the directions.

PRICES
For each listing, a suggested price indicates how much you can expect to spend. The price appears next to the address and contact details. Unless otherwise stated, the amount given in restaurant listings is the average price of a main course. For sights and attractions, we indicate the cost of a regular full-price ticket.

FESTIVALS & EVENTS
Amsterdam hosts many festivals, which are held throughout the city, especially during the summer.

LEGEND

● >> SIGHTS & ATTRACTIONS   ● >> SHOPPING
● >> FOOD & DRINK   ● >> MORE TO EXPLORE
✺ >> WALK HIGHLIGHT

Rollende Keukens—May and June (www.rollendekeukens.nl)
During this festival, the Westergasterrein and Westerpark turn into one giant
outdoor restaurant with food trucks, live music, and lots of finger food.

Amsterdam Roots—June (www.amsterdamroots.nl)
This world music and culture festival features around 60 concerts each year at
different locations throughout the city, plus the Roots Open Air festival in
Oosterpark.

ITs Festival Amsterdam—June and July (www.itsfestivalamsterdam.com)
A new generation of national and international performing artists presents their
graduation show performances at the International Theater School Festival.

Amsterdamse Bostheater—June, July, and August (www.bostheater.nl)
Outdoor performances, including theater (Shakespeare and other classics),
concerts, and children's shows are held in the Amsterdamse Bos (Amsterdam's
largest wooded park).

Summer in the Tolhuistuin—June, July, and August (www.tolhuistuin.nl)
This cultural festival in North Amsterdam, in Tolhuistuin Park, features an
outdoor stage, music, a wooden dance floor, and good food.

Keti Koti Festival—July 1 (www.ketikotiamsterdam.nl)
This festival is a celebration and remembrance of the abolition of slavery in the
former Dutch colonies, with an exuberant music party in Oosterpark.

Over het IJ Festival—July (www.overhetij.nl)
This is a pop-up theater festival in Amsterdam-Noord that features
performances at various locations, including the NDSM Wharf area.

Julidans—July (www.julidans.nl)
Performances take place throughout the city, from West to Zuidoost, during this
renowned festival of international contemporary dance.

Appelsap—last Sunday of July (www.appelsap.net)
This is a music festival in Oosterpark with hip-hop, urban, soul, and contemporary jazz.

Kwaku Summer Festival—July and August (www.kwakufestival.nl)
This multicultural festival takes place over four consecutive weekends in Bijlmerpark.

Grachtenfestival—August (www.grachtenfestival.nl)
Classical concerts are held at special locations on and near the canals in the city, the IJ waterfront, and in Noord.

Amsterdam Gay Pride—early August (www.amsterdampride.nl)
The largest gay event in the Netherlands, this festival features cultural and sporting activities, parties, and the flamboyant canal parade.

Parade—first half of August (www.deparade.nl)
This traveling outdoor theater festival in Martin Luther King Park showcases unique (and surprising) theater, music, and dance.

Magneet Festival—August (www.magneetfestival.nl)
Two weekends revolve around all things creative with crazy themes and a mix of music, theater, and art at the tip of the Zeeburgereiland.

Uitmarkt—last weekend of August (www.uitmarkt.nl)
A sneak preview of Amsterdam's upcoming cultural season, featuring performances, festivities, and market stalls at locations such as Museumplein and Leidseplein.

IDFA—November (www.idfa.nl)
The International Documentary Film Festival Amsterdam screens the best documentaries.

PUBLIC HOLIDAYS

In addition to Easter, Ascension Day, and Pentecost (whose dates vary each year), the Dutch celebrate the following official national holidays:

January 1 > New Year's Day
April 27 > King's Day
May 5 > Liberation Day
December 25 & 26 > Christmas

HAVE ANY TIPS?

Shops and restaurants in Amsterdam come and go fairly regularly. We do our best to keep the walks and contact details as up to date as possible. We also do our best to update the print edition often. However, if there is a place you can't find or if you have any other comments or tips, please let us know via email at info@momedia.nl.

TRANSPORTATION

Amsterdam is most easily reached from other European destinations by **train.** Exiting Amsterdam Centraal Station takes you directly into the city center. If you come by **car,** it's best to use a parking lot if you want to **park** in the Center. Parking rates on the street vary, depending on the district—from €1.40-€5 per hour. The closer to the Center you are, the higher the rates. Day tickets are also available. If you want to keep costs down, head for **P+R (Park & Ride)** from Amsterdam Arena, Sloterdijk train station, VU Medisch Centrum, Bos en Lommer, Olympisch Stadion, and Zeeburg. The rate is €8 per 24 hours (with a maximum stay of 96 hours).

The Amsterdam transport authority (GVB) will provide you with a P+R chip card for travel to the city center by tram, bus, or metro. From Sloterdijk and Arena, you will be given a train ticket to travel into the city center. Check the website www.iamsterdam.com/en/visiting/plan-your-trip/getting-around/parking for details.

You will need an **OV chipkaart** (smart card for public transport) with credit when traveling around Amsterdam. You can buy one at the machines in the train and subway stations, or you can buy an hour or day ticket on the tram, although this is generally more expensive. See www.ov-chipkaart.nl.

In the city center, the **tram** is your best option. Amsterdam has 15 tram lines, most of which depart from Centraal Station to the city's various districts. The **bus** is a good option if you're heading further out. There are special bus services from Centraal Station at night. Check www.gvb.nl for details.

Metro lines 53 and 54 connect Amsterdam Centraal Station with the Zuidoost area. Line 51 runs from Centraal Station via Buitenveldert to Amstelveen, and line 50 takes you from Amsterdam Sloterdijk station via Station Zuid to Gein. **Taxis** can be hailed on the street, and you'll find various taxi stands in the city center. You can always catch a taxi from Centraal Station. The best-known taxi company is TCA (tel. 020-7777777). The initial rate is €2.89 plus €2.12 per kilometer and €0.35 per minute. Make sure the driver observes the rules. You'll see bright yellow electric taxis, too, which are clean, silent, and resemble London cabs. In the Center, try a **bicycle taxi** for €1 per person per 3 minutes.

Real tourists take the **"hop-on, hop-off" boat** (with four lines and 20 stops). The boats navigate the canals and stop near the most important museums, shopping areas, and places of interest. A day ticket (€22) allows you to hop on and off all lines for the entire day. Evening tours are an option as well (reserve at www.canal.nl). Or take a trip with one of the **canal boats** departing from the Rokin. You'll also have nice views from the **"hop-on, hop-off" bus** (12 stops). A one-day ticket is €18 (www.citysightseeingamsterdam.nl).

BIKING

If you really want to experience Amsterdam and get around fast, hop on a bike. There are lovely cycling paths throughout the city, and it's a great way to explore the suburbs. You can also take your bike on the ferry and cycle around Amsterdam-Noord. The signs for cyclists are everywhere—look for the white signs with red letters. You can also buy maps of various cycling routes at the VVV tourist office at the Centraal train station.

Amsterdam is, of course, a cyclist's city, so most drivers are aware of the many cyclists on the road. But do be careful—it can get really hectic and busy, especially in the Center around Dam Square. As a cyclist, remember to watch out for pedestrians, other cyclists (visitors from abroad are not used to cycling here), buses, trams, and cars. Follow the rules of the road, even if most Amsterdammers don't, and, most importantly, steer clear of the tram tracks. A bell is highly recommended.

Bicycles can be rented from many places around Amsterdam, but first check if your hotel has them for free. If not, you can try **Macbike** (www.macbike.nl) or **Yellowbike** (www.yellowbike.nl). Both offer particularly nice guided tours in and around Amsterdam. If you really want to make a special afternoon of it, hop on a vintage **Velox bike** (www.veloxbikes.nl) and cycle around Amsterdam-Noord to picturesque Waterland, where a farmer will welcome you to Zunderdorp and invite you to milk the cows with him. Enjoy a fresh glass of milk afterward, which is a typically Dutch thing to do. The farmer's tour takes two and half hours and costs €29.50.

Do you live in the Netherlands? If so, you can arrange an **OV-fiets** season ticket (www.ns.nl/en/door-to-door/ov-fiets) before you visit Amsterdam. This free ticket is linked to your OV chipkaart and allows you to rent a bike at nearly every train station (including Amsterdam Centraal) for €3.85 a day. You can take two bikes at a time per ticket.

TOP 10   RESTAURANTS

| **TOP 10** | **MUSEUMS** |

1 Enjoy unusual films and exhibitions at **EYE** > p. 125

2 The renovated **Rijksmuseum** is a must-visit > p. 62

3 Explore worlds and cultures at **Tropenmuseum** > p. 102

4 **Tassenmuseum Hendrikje:** handbag history > Herengracht 573

5 View amazing images at **Foam** photography museum > p. 25

6 There's plenty to do at action museum **NEMO** > p. 136

7 Travel back in time at the **Scheepvaartmuseum** > p. 122

8 Visit the **Hermitage** for treasures from around the world > p. 22

9 Admire the Amsterdam School architectural style at **Museum Het Schip** > p. 85

10 Learn about resistance during WWII at the **Verzetsmuseum** > p. 102

1 Get a good start at **The Breakfast Club** > p. 69

2 Have a peaceful wander around scenic **Prinseneiland** > p. 42

3 Sit back and relax on the waterfront at **Hangar** > p. 129

4 A Sunday morning concert at The **Concertgebouw** > p. 77

5 Visit the beautiful greenhouses at **Hortus Botanicus** > p. 117

6 Grab an afternoon drink on lively theater street **Nes** > p. 37

7 Browse the lovely little boutiques on **Utrechtsestraat** > p. 21

8 Take a bike ride through the **Amsterdamse Bos** > p. 138

9 Sample beers outdoors under the windmill at **Brouwerij 't IJ** > p. 126

10 Catch a film at **The Movies,** Amsterdam's oldest cinema > p. 57

TOP 10	NIGHTLIFE

1   **Paradiso** is Amsterdam's pop temple > Weteringschans 6-8

2   **Pacific Parc** has live music and DJs > p. 90

3   **Club AIR** knows how to throw a good party > Amstelstraat 24

4   For live jazz head to **Bourbon Street** > Leidsekruisstraat 6-8

5   Visit **Brouwerij De Prael** for beer tasting in the Red Light District > p. 37

6   **Canvas** offers dancing with a view > Wibautstraat 150

7   Watch films in style at **Tuschinski** > Reguliersbreestraat 26-34

8   **Melkweg** hosts great parties and concerts > Lijnbaansgracht 234A

9   **Tolhuistuin** always has a diverse program > p. 137

10   **The Waterhole** is for rock lovers > Korte Leidsedwarsstraat 49

CENTER

ABOUT THE WALK

This is the most touristy walk in the book, featuring places for which Amsterdam is most famous, such as the Red Light District, multicultural Zeedijk, and the Canal District. Varied and with a rich history, this walk leads through both busy and quieter areas. It's quite long, so you can also split it in two by walking back down the Oudezijds Achterburgwal, after you've gone halfway, to return to the starting point.

THE NEIGHBORHOODS

If you arrive by train at Centraal Station, you'll step right out into Amsterdam's vibrant center. Many tourists get no further than Damrak, the Red Light District, and the Kalverstraat. But the Center has a lot more to offer. Amsterdam owes much of its fame to the **Canal District,** which was designated a UNESCO World Heritage Site in 2010. During the 17th century (the Netherlands' Golden Age), monumental buildings were built with large inner courtyards, transforming the Kalverstraat from a muddy livestock market into a chic shopping street. Although today it's full of many of the usual chains, it's still possible to find some beautiful spots around the Kalverstraat, such as the **Begijnhof, Beurs van Berlage,** the **Royal Palace** (Koninklijk Paleis) on Dam Square, and the **Amsterdam Museum.** Around the large shopping streets, you can also find many small streets with boutiques and specialty stores.

Wandering past the canals with their stately mansions, it's easy to forget that Amsterdam dates not from the Golden Age but from much earlier and was granted city rights in 1342. From modern maps, you can see how the medieval city was built around the port. There was once open sea where the Centraal train station now stands. Today, only the stretch of water next to Damrak remains.

The world's most famous red-light district, the **Wallen,** forms the oldest part of the city. Although you may regularly stumble across drunken bachelor parties,

🔟 The **Magere Brug** (Skinny Bridge) is one of the most attractive drawbridges in Amsterdam. It's beautifully lit at night. The Mager ladies were two wealthy sisters who lived on either side of the Amstel, and allegedly built the original bridge in 1670 in order to visit each other more easily. It's more likely that the bridge got its name simply because it's so narrow.
Amstel, between Keizersgracht and Prinsengracht (extension of Kerkstraat),
Tram 2, 4, 11, 12 Prinsengracht

🔟 Photography enthusiasts can indulge at **Foam,** Amsterdam's photography museum. Alongside works by big names such as Erwin Olaf and Jim Goldberg are displays by lesser-known talent. There are usually three or four exhibitions on at the same time.
Keizersgracht 609, www.foam.org, tel. 020-5516500, open Sat-Wed 10am-6pm,
Thur-Fri 10am-9pm, entrance €10, Tram 2, 4, 11, 12 Keizersgracht

⑲ **De Munt** (The Mint) is a remnant of the Regulierspoort, a city gate that was built in 1487 and was rebuilt after a fire in 1620. It was part of the medieval city wall. The tower got its name during the French occupation when it was no longer possible to transport silver and gold to the mints in Dordrecht and Enkhuizen.
Muntplein, not open to the public, Tram 24 Muntplein

⑳ The **Oudemanhuispoort** is a covered passageway running from Oudezijds Achterburgwal to Kloveniersburgwal. The gate used to lead to the Oude Mannen- en Vrouwe Gasthuis (Old Men's and Women's house). Nowadays it leads onto the Binnengasthuis Terrein, an enclosed area that is part of the University of Amsterdam. The passageway houses a used books market.
Oudemanhuispoort, open book market Mon-Sat 9am-5pm, free, Tram 24 Muntplein

㉑ In the middle ages, the **Begijnhof** was a place where single, religious women could live together, nurse the sick, and offer classes. Today it's an oasis of calm in Amsterdam's busy downtown district.
Begijnhof (use entrance gate at Spui), www.begijnhofamsterdam.nl, open daily 9am-5pm, free, Tram 2, 11, 12 Spui, Tram 4, 14, 24 Rokin, Metro 52 Rokin

㉗ Unsurprisingly, you can learn all about Amsterdam at the **Amsterdam Museum.** Seven centuries of history are recounted through stories of city life, old movies, photos, sound recordings, and paintings.
Nieuwezijds Voorburgwal 357 and Kalverstraat 92, www.amsterdammuseum.nl, tel. 020-5231822, open daily 10am-5pm, entrance €13.50, Tram 2, 11, 12 Spui, Tram 4, 14, 24 Rokin, Metro 52 Rokin

㉙ Originally serving as the city hall, this building assumed its current function as the **Koninklijk Paleis** (Royal Palace) in 1808. It's still used for ceremonial occasions—Queen Beatrix abdicated here in 2013. The interior is beautiful, thanks to the restored chandeliers, furniture, and artistic masterpieces.
Dam 1, www.paleisamsterdam.nl, tel. 020-6204060, open daily 11am-5pm (closed during official engagements), entrance €10, Tram 2, 4, 11, 12, 13, 14, 17, 24 Dam

㉚ The **Nieuwe Kerk** (New Church) was built in the 14th century because the Old Church could no longer accommodate the growing number of churchgoers. The official inaugurations of seven generations of the royal family of Orange-Nassau have taken place here. Crown Prince Willem-Alexander married Maxima in this church and was sworn in here as the king of the Netherlands on April 30, 2013. Great photo and art exhibitions are regularly held here.
Dam 12, www.nieuwekerk.nl, tel. 020-6386909, opening times vary, entrance fee varies, Tram 2, 4, 11, 12, 13, 14, 17, 24 Dam

㉝ Grain, securities, and commodities were originally traded at the **Beurs van Berlage.** The architect, Berlage, was inspired by Italian architecture. He longed for a more just society in which exchange trading was abolished. No longer a stock market, the building now hosts conferences, concerts, and exhibitions. On Saturdays, you can take a tour reviewing Berlage's career as an architect.
Damrak 243, www.beursvanberlage.nl, tel. 020-5304141, weekly tour on Sat 10:30am-noon, tour €14.50 including drinks, Tram 2, 4, 11, 12, 13, 14, 17, 24 Dam

34 The **Oude Kerk** (Old Church) is Amsterdam's oldest building. The church was probably originally a wooden chapel. The first stones were laid around 1306, and the church gradually assumed its current form over the subsequent centuries. Exhibitions and concerts are regularly held here.

Oudekerksplein 23, www.oudekerk.nl, tel. 020-6258284, open Mon-Sat 10am-5:30pm, Sun 1pm-5pm, entrance €7.50, Tram 2, 4, 11, 12, 13, 14, 17, 24 Dam

37 The attic of this canal house hides a Catholic church from the 16th century. At that time, the official religion was Calvinism, and non-Calvinists were allowed to hold services only in places that were unrecognizable as churches. And so the church of **Ons' Lieve Heer op Solder** (Our Dear Lord in the Attic) came to be and can now be visited as a museum.

Oudezijds Voorburgwal 40, www.opsolder.nl, tel. 020-6246604, open Mon-Sat 10am-5pm, Sun and holidays 1pm-5pm, entrance €8, Tram 2, 4, 11, 12, 13, 14, 17, 24, 26 Centraal Station, Metro 51, 52, 53, 54 Centraal Station

WIJS BIER

* Blonde Poes.
* Kopi Luwak.

FOOD & DRINK

❶ You wouldn't expect to find a place as cozy as **Dwaze Zaken** (Foolish Matters) opposite Centraal Station, but you'll soon feel completely at ease in this arty café. The menu offers drinks as well as vegetarian, organic, fair trade, and locally produced food options. On Monday nights, you can have a potluck for just €6.90. The café also often has live jazz performances and temporary exhibitions.

Prins Hendrikkade 50, www.dwazezaken.nl, tel. 020-6124175, open Mon-Thur 9am-11pm, Fri-Sat 9am-midnight, price €18, Tram 2, 4, 11, 12, 13, 14, 17, 24, 26 Centraal Station

❸ Home-roasted coffee beans are in, though that's nothing new, as **Hofje van Wijs** can testify—the business has been importing coffee and tea for more than 200 years. In the peaceful courtyard, the bustle of the Zeedijk seems far away, and you can sample what used to be luxury beverages, which are now consumed daily.

Zeedijk 43, www.hofjevanwijs.nl, tel. 020-6240436, open Tue-Sun noon-11pm, coffee from €2.10, tea from €3, Tram 2, 4, 11, 12, 13, 14, 17, 24, 26 Centraal Station, Metro 51, 52, 53, 54 Centraal Station

❹ Somewhat hidden between the many Asian restaurants and shops on Zeedijk you'll find **Sugar & Spice Bakery.** As the name suggests, this cozy coffeehouse offers a variety of many different treats, both sweet and savory. It's a welcome change in this old Amsterdam neighborhood. Their flavorful sweet-and-savory brunch platters come highly recommended, wand they also have vegan options.

Zeedijk 75, www.sugarspicebakery-amsterdam.nl, tel. 065-5701765, open Sun-Mon & Sat 10am-6pm, Tue-Fri 9am-6pm, brunch platter €17, Tram 2, 4, 11, 12, 13, 14, 17, 24, 26 Centraal Station, Metro 51, 53, 54 Nieuwmarkt

❺ **Thai Bird** is a known fixture on Zeedijk. Don't come here expecting an elaborate dining experience that will last all evening. But if a fast and tasty meal is what you're after, then this is the place. This popular restaurant is so tiny, it can feel rather crowded. But what it lacks in space, it certainly makes up for in charm. You will probably need to wait awhile for a table, but the fresh and delicious Thai dishes served here are well worth it.

Zeedijk 77, www.thaibird.nl, tel. 020-4206289, open Sun & Thur-Sat 1pm-10:30pm, Mon-Wed 1pm-10pm, mains from €13, Tram 2, 4, 11, 12, 13, 14, 17, 24, 26 Centraal Station, Metro 51, 53, 54 Nieuwmarkt

❾ De Waag originally formed part of the medieval city walls. The building, which dates to before 1425, used to be called Saint Anthony's Gate. In the 17th century, it was converted into a weighing house. Since then, it has housed a guild, museum, fire station, and the anatomical theater that formed the setting for Rembrandt's painting *The Anatomy Lesson of Dr. Nicolaes Tulp.* Today, you can lunch, snack, or dine at the restaurant **In de Waag.** There's a lovely view from the outdoor seating area of the imposing Weigh House.

Nieuwmarkt 4, www.indewaag.nl, tel. 020-4227772, open daily 9am-4pm, 5pm-10:30pm, from €23, Tram 2, 4, 11, 12, 13, 14, 17, 24, 26 Centraal Station, Metro 51, 53, 54 Nieuwmarkt

⓫ Pizza for breakfast? Then head to **Betty Blue.** Alongside standards such as pancakes and fried eggs, the menu also features breakfast pizzas. This little gem on the corner of Snoekjessteeg is a great place for breakfast, brunch, or lunch. And with an extensive selection of pies and cakes, you are spoilt for choice. Their outside terrace is the perfect place to relax and watch city life pass you by—a quiet and peaceful spot in the middle of a buzzing neighborhood.

Snoekjessteeg 1, www.bettyblueamsterdam.nl, tel. 020-8100924, open Sun 9:30am-6pm, Mon-Sat 8:30am-6pm, from €8, Tram 14 Waterlooplein, Metro 51, 53, 54 Waterlooplein

㉒ Just try walking past the window of **De Laatste Kruimel** (The Last Crumb) without your mouth watering. Tantalizing cheesecakes, moist brownies, and scrumptious cakes are all there to tempt you—and they are all the more delicious when you know that everything is made with natural ingredients. If you're lucky, there might be a seat along the water, though it's also a pleasure to sit inside with a view of the kitchen.

Langebrugsteeg 4, www.delaatstekruimel.nl, tel. 020-4230499, open Mon-Sat 8am-8pm, Sun 9am-8pm, slice of cake €3.50, Tram 2, 4, 11, 12, 13, 14, 17, 24 Dam

23 Hidden away in Taksteeg—an alleyway in the middle of the busy city center, between Kalverstraat and Rokin—you'll find **Gartine:** a hole in the wall that is one of Amsterdam's best-kept secrets. Many of their fruits and vegetables are freshly picked from their own garden—and you can taste the difference. Try the nettle cheese on sourdough bread with homemade chutney or the ginger and pear pie. This is also the perfect place for high tea. Remember to make reservations if you come here for lunch because they're always packed.
Taksteeg 7, www.gartine.nl, tel. 020-3204132, open Wed-Sat 10am-6pm, lunch €10, high tea starting €18.95, Tram 4, 14, 24 Rokin, Metro 52

24 De Kalvertoren shopping center is a cut above the rest, which is reflected in restaurant **Blue°.** Making the most of the location, there's a beautiful view through the glass facade from virtually every table. Take the glass elevator to the top for a sandwich or a glass of wine, and take a walk around the restaurant to view the city on all sides.
Singel 457, www.blue-amsterdam.nl, tel. 020-4273901, open Mon 11am-6:30pm, Tue-Wed & Fri-Sat 10am-6:30pm, Thur 10am-9pm, Sun noon-6:30pm, sandwich €7.50, Tram 2, 11, 12 Koningsplein, Tram 24 Muntplein

WALK 1 > CENTER

㉕ For the very best fries in town, head to **Vlaams Friethuis** (Flemish fries shop), where 55 years of experience have certainly paid off. Choose from 25 sauces—from mayonnaise to samurai sauce, and from ketchup to yellow curry. Voetboogstraat 33, www.vleminckxdesausmeester.nl, tel. 020-6246075, open Sun-Mon noon-7pm, Tue-Wed & Fri-Sat 11am-7pm, Thur 11am-9pm, fries and sauce €2.80, Tram 24 Muntplein, Tram 2, 11, 12 Koningsplein

㉘ At **Stadspaleis** you are spoiled for healthy choices like wraps, salads, and soups—all made with pure ingredients and fair-trade products. Try the organic Flemish fries with homemade tartar sauce, a delicious accompaniment to the organic burger. It's healthy yet scrumptious eating in this teeny-tiny lunchroom. Nieuwezijds Voorburgwal 289, www.stadspaleis.com, tel. 020-6256542, open daily 11am-7pm, sandwich €6.50, Tram 2, 11, 12 Spui, Tram 4, 14, 24 Rokin, Metro 52 Rokin

㉜ The chocolate served at **Metropolitan Deli** is reminiscent of the romantic film *Chocolat*. It's a dangerous place—here they do anything and everything with chocolate. Try the homemade Italian ice cream, too. The deli sometimes organizes tastings. Warmoesstraat 135, www.metropolitandeli.nl, tel. 020-3301955, open daily 9am-1am, chocolate tasting €7.95 (minimum of four people), Tram 2, 4, 11, 12, 13, 14, 17, 24 Dam

㉟ Italian restaurants abound in the center of Amsterdam, though the quality of the pasta often leaves much to be desired. At **Pasta Pasta,** they understand that making pasta is an art in its own right. The pasta is purchased fresh from the market every morning. The result: handmade pasta topped with fresh ingredients. Warmoesstraat 49, www.pasta-pasta.nl, tel. 020-3311199, open Sun-Thur 11am-midnight, Fri-Sat 11am-2am, from €5, Tram 2, 4, 11, 12, 13, 14, 17, 24 Dam

㊳ Taste the atmosphere of old Amsterdam at café **Int Aepjen** (Old Dutch meaning "at the monkey"). The Dutch saying *in de aap gelogeerd* (literally, "stayed at the monkey," meaning to be in a bad situation) apparently originated here. The story goes that during the 15th century, if guests couldn't pay their bill, the owner would accept payment in kind—in the form of monkeys that sailors often brought with them. Apparently, the monkeys often had fleas, so if someone was spotted walking along the seafront scratching vigorously, it was said, "He must have stayed at the monkey!"

Zeedijk 1, tel. 020-6268401, open Sun-Thur noon-1am, Fri-Sat noon-3am, drink €3, Tram 2, 4, 11, 12, 13, 14, 17, 24, 26 Centraal Station, Metro 51, 52, 53, 54 Centraal Station

SHOPPING

6 Toko Dun Yong is by far the largest Asian shop in the city and one of the oldest, dating back 60 years. You'll find more than just food and drink in the building's six stories—this is the place for all things Chinese, from cookware to books, music, and porcelain. Check out the restaurant on the second floor for some good noodle soup.

Stormsteeg 9, www.dunyong.com, tel. 020-6221763, open Mon-Fri 9am-7pm, Sat 9am-6pm, Sun noon-6pm, Tram 2, 4, 11, 12, 13, 14, 17, 24, 26 Centraal Station, Metro 51, 52, 53, 54 Centraal Station

7 Asia is not only a source of ancient culinary traditions but also various new trends. **Asia Station** collects all the novelties the continent has to offer—from bubble tea to beautiful Asian-style dresses and from gadgets you've never seen before to cosmetics by special Asian brands.

Zeedijk 100, www.asiastation.nl, tel. 020-3032628, open daily 11:30am-9pm, Tram 2, 4, 11, 12, 13, 14, 17, 24, 26 Centraal Station, Metro 51, 52, 53, 54 Centraal Station

10 Bis! is a must for all lovers of vintage clothing, with a whopping three shops filled to the brim with clothes, shoes, hats, and accessories. They sell unique fashion items—whether you're looking for a special 1950s evening gown or a funky pantsuit from the '70s. One of the three shops is dedicated to army and navy apparel. They also have a good selection of menswear.

Sint Antoniesbreestraat 25a, www.bis-vintage.nl, tel. 020-6203467, open Sun noon-5pm, Mon noon-6pm, Tue-Sat 11am-6pm, Tram 14 Waterlooplein, Metro 51, 53, 54 Waterlooplein

13 Located behind the Town Hall and Music Theater, the market on **Waterlooplein** has 300 stalls selling mostly secondhand wares. "If it's not for sale here, then it doesn't exist," as the saying goes. The market's not cheap, but it's still fun to visit.

Waterlooplein, waterlooplein.amsterdam, open Mon-Sat 9am-6pm, Tram 14 Waterlooplein, Metro 51, 53, 54 Waterlooplein

14 Handmade buffalo leather bags, Japanese crockery, or sketchbooks from handmade paper. If you're on the hunt for an original present for yourself or a friend, **Biec** is the place to be. Time flies in this curiosity shop because there is so much to see and choose from. They focus on sustainable products from all over the world, and there is something to be had for everyone.

Staalstraat 28, https://biec.nl, tel. 020-2620316, open Sun-Mon noon-6:30pm, Tue-Sat 11am-6:30pm, Tram 24 Muntplein

⑰ MaisonNL is a fun concept store that constantly changes its stock. You can find anything here from Scandinavian clothing to home accessories made of natural materials and lingerie from Amsterdam Love Stories clothing.
Utrechtsestraat 118, www.maisonnl.com, tel. 020-4285183, open Mon 1pm-6pm, Tue-Sat 10:30am-6pm, Sun 1pm-5pm, Tram 2, 4, 11, 12 Prinsengracht di-za 10.30-18.00, zo 13.00-17.00, tram 4 prinsengracht

MORE TO EXPLORE

㉑ At first sight, **Nes** might look a bit drab, but don't be fooled—in the evenings and on Sundays, this street comes to life with animated theater-goers heading for Frascati (the oldest theater on the street), the Comedy Theater, Brakke Grond, or the Torpedo Theater. While here, take a look down Gebed zonder End (Prayer without End), an alley that refers to one of the many monasteries located in the city during the Middle Ages.
Nes, Tram 2, 4, 11, 12, 13, 14, 17, 24 Dam

㉛ **W139** is an internationally renowned exhibition space and haven for fine art. It's a place where artists can experiment. Festivals, concerts, dance performances, and other activities are regularly held here. Drop in and be surprised by the variety of contemporary art projects in this industrial-style gallery.
Warmoesstraat 139, www.w139.nl, tel. 020-6229434, open daily noon-6pm, free, Tram 2, 4, 11, 12, 13, 14, 17, 24 Dam

㊱ You can now find **Brouwerij De Prael** on a street formerly known as de Bierkade (beer quay). Take a tour through the brewery and then hang out at the bar with beers named after heroes from the Dutch tears-in-your-beer-type ballads. The tasting room also doubles as a learning center for people with a history of mental illness who find it hard to find work.
Oudezijds Armsteeg 26 (Proeflokaal), www.deprael.nl, tel. 020-4084469, open tasting room Mon-Wed noon-midnight, Thur-Sat noon-1am, Sun noon-11pm, tours every hour Mon-Fri 1pm-6pm, Sat 1pm-5pm, Sun 2pm-5pm, tour €8.50, tasting room €10, tour and tasting €17.50, Tram 2, 4, 11, 12, 13, 14, 17, 24, 26 Centraal Station

JORDAAN & NEGEN STRAATJES

ABOUT THE WALK

This walk leads you past historical canal houses and shops. You'll stroll down the charming Haarlemmerstraat to the lovely, quiet Prinseneiland and on to the lively Jordaan with its many cafés. The Negen Straatjes (Nine Little Streets) are an absolute must for any shopaholic. The walk is worth it, even you don't like shopping—this neighborhood is in the most beautiful part of town, with scenic views of many bridges and canals.

THE NEIGHBORHOODS

The **Jordaan** is considered Amsterdam's most pleasant neighborhood. Previously a blue-collar quarter, it has been increasingly gentrified over the years, now that anyone with money is willing to fork it over for a property. The quaint streets and scenic canals are now dominated by yuppies on designer cargo bikes and affluent expats.

It's easy to forget that this neighborhood used to be far removed from the riches of the canal belt. The Jordaan was constructed in 1612 for workers and immigrants. It became increasingly impoverished from the 19th century onward, until the 1970s when the municipality began extensive rejuvenation. Since then, the Jordaan has been transformed from a working-class neighborhood into an expensive area, home to the well-educated.

It might seem as though the special atmosphere of yesteryear—of folk songs, pubs, and tacky jokes told in the broad Amsterdam dialect—are a thing of the past. Trendy shops and living spaces now occupy the buildings that once housed traditional businesses. But the good old days is far from forgotten. On **Johnny Jordaanplein,** for example, the Dutch *levenslied* (tear-jerking beer ballad) is honored. Like the Jordaan, the **Negen Straatjes** have also become a must-see for any Amsterdam visitor. And for good reason—the area is lined with unique boutiques, delicatessens, home decor stores, and lovely cafés. The nine streets run parallel to one another between the canals and are considered Amsterdam's finest shopping district.

SHORT ON TIME? HERE ARE THE HIGHLIGHTS:

8 PRINSENEILAND + 13 APPLE PIE AT WINKEL 43 + 17 HET OUD-HOLLANDSCH SNOEPWINKELTJE + 24 CHOCOLATERIE POMPADOUR + 34 ANNE FRANK HUIS

TIPS
// A must for shopaholics
// Nice on Mondays when there's a market
// Lots of cozy, traditional Dutch pubs

casa de **anne frank**
Um museu com uma história

JORDAAN & NEGEN STRAATJES

WALK 2 DESCRIPTION (approx. 5.5 mi/9 km)

Start on Haarlemmerstraat ❶ ❷. Bear left for the West-Indisch Huis ❸ and keep going ❹ ❺ ❻ ❼. Turn right onto Buiten Oranjestraat. Walk under the railway and on Hendrik Jonkerplein head for Bickersgracht. Take the first bridge left and walk left over Prinseneiland ⓼. Turn right at the end of the street, then right again onto Galgenstraat, and then left over the water. Turn left again, under the railway and cross the road until you get to Haarlemmerdijk. Turn left ❾, right, and right again onto Vinkenstraat ❿. Turn left at the end, then left again onto Brouwersgracht. Cross the first bridge, turn left, and walk alongside the water to Café Thijssen ⓫. Turn right onto Lindengracht and left via the Noorderkerkstraat to the Noordermarkt ⓬ ⓭. Turn right onto Westerstraat and take the first right. When you arrive at Boomstraat, take a left. Cross Tweede Boomdwarsstraat diagonally to Karthuizerstraat ⓮. Walk left onto Tichelstraat and past ⓯ ⓰ ⓱. Cross Egelantiersgracht and go left until you reach Prinsengracht. Turn right and take the first right to check out some special T-shirts ⓲. Walk down Nieuwe Leliestraat, take the second street left and then take the first right onto Bloemgracht. Follow the street to the next bridge, cross over, turn right onto Bloemstraat, then take the first left. Continue walking to Elandsgracht, then turn left for Palladio ⓳ and to reach Holland's famous folk singers ⓴. Turn right onto Prinsengracht, right again onto Oude Looiersstraat, then the first left. Cross the canal, turn right to reach Lijnbaansgracht, then turn left. Head over the canal, turn left, then right for the Turnzaal ㉑. Turn around and go via Raamplein to Passeerdersgracht ㉒ until you reach Prinsengracht. Turn left and take the first bridge on the right for Negen Straatjes ㉓ ㉔ ㉕. Cross to the other side of Herengracht and turn left for a liqueur ㉖. Cross Herengracht again. Walk down Prinsengracht along the right side of the canal. Take the first right for good food ㉗ ㉘ ㉙ and great shopping ㉚ ㉛. Walk down Singel on the left, and turn left again. Walk through the shopping arcade and cross the road at Westermarkt for some noteworthy sights ㉜ ㉝ ㉞. Continue over Prinsengracht and turn right onto Leliegracht. Finish the walk with dinner ㉟ ㊱ ㊲.

SIGHTS & ATTRACTIONS

West-Indisch Huis, the former head office of the Dutch West India Company, which participated in the Atlantic slave trade, is the place where its directors decided to build a fort on the island of Manhattan that was to later become New York.
Herenmarkt 99, not open to the public, Tram 2, 4, 11, 12, 13, 14, 17, 24, 26 Centraal Station, Metro 51, 52, 53, 54 Centraal Station

This often-overlooked part of Amsterdam is quite beautiful. The Dutch West India Company used the neighborhood's shipyards and warehouses to store herring, grain, tobacco, wine, salt, anchovies, cat skins, pitch, and tar. In the first half of the 20th century, **Prinseneiland** fell out of favor and was almost deserted until after World War II when it was rediscovered by artists. The oldest 17th century houses are at numbers 269 and 517.
Prinseneiland, Tram 3 Zoutkeetsgracht

The real Jordaan still survives in places such as the **Jordaanmuseum,** where you'll also find an exhibition about life in the Jordaan. In this nursing home, you can learn more about the district's many upheavals, street life, theaters, and artists. If your Dutch is up to par, try and have a chat with one of the residents, and if you're lucky, you'll hear all about "the good old days." The people behind this initiative would like to purchase the property to house their collection, so feel free to give a donation.
Vinkenstraat 185, www.jordaanmuseum.nl, tel. 020-6244695, open daily 10am-5pm, free, Tram 3 Haarlemmerplein

The icons of the Jordaan's popular folk songs can be found on **Johnny Jordaanplein,** which is actually part of Elandsgracht. The feelings Johnny Jordaan captures in his hit song "Geef mij maar Amsterdam" ("I prefer Amsterdam over any other city") are almost tangible around his statue and those of fellow Jordaan singers. The rumor is that a sculpture of Johnny Jordaan's nephew, Willy Alberti, will soon join his uncle on the square.
Elandsgracht, Tram 5, 7, 19 Elandsgracht

㉑ The Neo-Renaissance **Turnzaal** (Gymnasium) was built in 1887 after gymnastics became compulsory in Amsterdam's primary schools in 1862. In addition to a large gymnasium and an outbuilding, there is also a caretaker's house and bartender's lodgings (there was a beer cellar in the basement). Since 1978 the building has been home to an educational youth theater, Jeugdtheater de Krakeling that also rents out the foyer, theater hall, and basement.
Nieuwe Passeerdersstraat 1, not open to the public, Tram 5, 7, 19 Elandsgracht

㉒ In the days before recruitment agencies and job centers, you had to come here if you were looking for work or workers. Founded in 1887, the **Arbeidsbeurs** (Labor Exchange) moved to this specially constructed building, designed in the Amsterdam School style, in 1918. Men entered on the left, women on the right. Eighty employees shared various jobs, with a clear division of labor not only between the genders but also between professional groups.
Passeerdersgracht 30, not open to the public, Tram 5, 7, 19 Elandsgracht

32 The 270-foot-high (85-meter-high) tower of the **Westerkerk** is the symbol of the Jordaan. Princess Beatrix of the Netherlands and Prince Claus were married in this 17th-century church on March 10, 1966. Weekly services are still held here.

Prinsengracht 281, www.westerkerk.nl, open Mon-Fri 10am-3pm, Sat 11am-3pm, free, Tram 13, 17 Westermarkt

33 It's estimated that 10,000 homosexuals were killed in concentration camps during World War II. The pink triangle they were forced to wear later became the symbol of the gay movement. The **Homomonument**'s three pink triangles symbolize the past (the triangle at street level, pointing to the Anne Frank House), present (the triangle in the water, pointing to the National Monument on the Dam), and future (the triangle above street level, pointing to the headquarters of gay rights group COC).

Westermarkt, www.homomonument.nl, Tram 13, 17 Westermarkt

At the world-famous **Anne Frank Huis,** you can visit the hiding place of the Frank family via the stairs behind the bookcase and view Anne's original diary. Arrive as early as possible—the lines are often very long.

Prinsengracht 263-237, www.annefrank.org, tel. 020-5567100, open Nov-Mar, Sun-Fri 9am-7pm, Sat 9am-9pm, Apr-Oct daily 9am-10pm, entrance €9, Tram 13, 17 Westermarkt

FOOD & DRINK

2 You're welcome in the early morning hours throughout the week at this slick café with Danish designer chairs and Dutch designer lamps. The chefs at **Vinnies Deli** work as much as possible with organic, fair trade, and eco-friendly products—by simply cooking with seasonal vegetables. All the ingredients, such as home-cooked granola and organic quinoa, are also for sale.

Haarlemmerstraat 46, vinnieshomepage.com, tel. 020-7713086 open Mon-Fri 7:30am-6pm, Sat 9am-6pm, Sun 9:30am-6pm, sandwich €8, Tram 2, 4, 11, 12, 13, 14, 17, 24, 26 Centraal Station, Metro 51, 52, 53, 54 Centraal Station

❹ The tiny cakes at **Petit Gâteau** look like works of art—almost too beautiful to eat. Almost, because they taste divine! The atmosphere is akin to a proper French patisserie in Paris. Everything is made on the premises, so you can watch every mouthwatering morsel as it's created. Beware though: before you know it, you'll be ordering seconds—just watching will be enough to make you hungry for more!

Haarlemmerstraat 80, petitgateau.nl, tel. 020-7371585, open daily 10am-6pm, from €4, Tram 2, 4, 11, 12, 13, 14, 17, 24, 26 Centraal Station, Metro 51, 52, 53, 54 Centraal Station

⓫ Where typical "Jordanees" (people born and raised in the Jordaan neighborhood) meets preppy—this is probably the best way to describe **Café Thijssen.** You'll feel right at home in this cozy bar where young and old from all walks of life mingle seamlessly. If you like a bit of buzz, come here in the evening, or on Saturdays when the weekly market is held. During the week, this is a great place to sit and read the paper or have a chat at the bar. The sandwich with Amsterdam *osseworst*—raw beef sausage—is not to be missed! In the summertime they offer some of the best outdoor seating in the Jordaan.

Brouwersgracht 107, www.cafethijssen.nl, tel. 020-6238994, open Sun 8am-midnight, Mon-Thur 8am-1am, Fri 8am-3am, Sat 7:30am-3am, Tram 13, 17 Westermarkt

🏶 **Winkel 43** (Shop 43) is a favorite hangout in the heart of the Jordaan for a drink or a bite to eat. The apple pie is particularly delicious here—many consider it to be the best in Amsterdam, but of course you can decide for yourself! In summer, the long, wooden tables outside are always busy. It's the ideal place to relax after a visit to the Noordermarkt on a Saturday or Monday.

Noordermarkt 43, www.winkel43.nl, tel. 020-6230223 open Mon 7am-1am, Tue-Thur 8am-1am, Fri 8am-3pm, Sat 7am-3pm, Sun 10am-1pm, apple pie with cream and coffee €5.80, Tram 3 Nieuwe Willemsstraat

⓯ This is one of those bars that most tourists will walk past. And that isn't such a bad thing because here you can enjoy the company of genuine locals. **Café de Tuin** is a no-nonsense place with the typical interior decor of an authentic "Jordanees" bar. The walls are filled with prints, the shelves are lined with

ornaments, and the vibe is great. If you manage to secure a place out front on a nice day, expect to be here for a while. This buzzing little street has lots to see.
Tweede Tuindwarsstraat 13, www.cafedetuin.nl, tel. 020-6244559, open Sun 11am-1am, Mon-Thur 10am-1am, Fri-Sat 10am-3am, from €8, Tram 3, 5 Marnixplein, Tram 13, 17 Westermarkt

16 If you've ever been to Northern Spain, you probably know what *pintxos* are: small slices of bread with a variety of toppings. This and much more can be found on the menu of **La Oliva.** Together with some great Spanish wines and incredibly friendly staff, this is the perfect place for a Spanish evening in the heart of the Jordaan. Expect unique flavor combinations—and if you love Spanish ham, this is the place to be.
Egelantiersstraat 122-124, www.laoliva.nl, tel. 020-3204316, open Sun-Wed noon-10pm, Thur-Sat noon-11pm, from €15, Tram 3, 5 Marnixplein, Tram 13, 17 Westermarkt

19 You won't find bottles hanging from the ceiling or rustic murals on the wall at restaurant **Palladio.** Instead, there are plenty of light, fresh flowers, chandeliers, and lovely outdoor seating. The menu may also be a little different from what you'd expect at an Italian restaurant—there are no pizzas, but homemade pasta and fresh vegetables, fish, and meat instead. Try the seafood special: a catch of the day from the Dutch Wadden Sea.

Elandsgracht 64, www.restaurantpalladio.nl, tel. 020-6277442, open Tue-Sun 6pm-10:30pm, pasta €14.50, Tram 5, 7, 19 Elandsgracht

㉗ Pluk offers healthy juices, salads, and sandwiches, as well as delicious cakes and pastries, all available to take away. On the upper floor of this lovely, light space you can enjoy an extensive lunch. In addition to food and drink, Pluk is a great place to shop if you're looking for an original gift. Cookbooks, vases, cups, and dish towels are just a few of the lovely goods.

Reestraat 19, www.pluk9straatjes.nl, open Mon-Sat 9am-6pm, Sun 10am-6pm, from €10, Tram 2, 4, 11, 12, 13, 14, 17, 24 Dam

㉘ With the advent of venues such as **Ree7,** pubs with good-quality menus—"gastropubs"—have arrived in Amsterdam. You'll find tasty, no-frills sandwiches at lunch, and spareribs, chicken satay, or burgers for dinner. Try to find a spot by the door or at the window—it's a great place to do some people watching.

Reestraat 7, www.ree7.nl, tel. 020-3307639, open daily 9am-6pm, from €17, Tram 2, 4, 11, 12, 13, 14, 17, 24 Dam

㉙ At **Screaming Beans,** they know their coffee—and it shows. Here coffee is brewed with the utmost precision and they use their own selection of beans, procured from small farmers and roasted in-house. They're always on the hunt for new flavors, and tasting is all part of the experience. Drip coffee is brewed at your table, and if you're not a big fan of the black gold there is a special selection of teas.

Hartenstraat 12, tel. 020-6260966, open Mon-Tue and Thur-Fri 8am-5pm, Wed 8am-6pm, Sat 9am-5pm, from €3.50, Tram 13, 17 Westermarkt

㉟ Vegan food is certainly not boring at **Vegabond,** thanks to owner Babet. The business is colorful and sells surprising vegan produce and meals, such as (mostly gluten-free) cupcakes, pizza, or sandwiches. Choose a spot overlooking the canal or browse through the products. Be sure to try the beer from Amsterdam microbrewery Oedipus!

Leliegracht 16, www.vegabond.nl, tel. 020-8468927, open Tue-Sat 11am-7pm, Sun noon-7pm, sandwich €5, Tram 13, 17 Westermarkt

36 The name of this restaurant, **De Luwte** (The Shelter) is no accident. It's wonderful to relax in this sheltered nook, situated on one of the Jordaan's idyllic canals. The menu is international with a nod to Mediterranean cuisine. If that doesn't whet your appetite, it's also nice to sit inside by the fireplace with a glass of red wine or sip a cocktail overlooking the canal.

Leliegracht 26, www.restaurantdeluwte.nl, tel. 020-6258548, open daily 6pm-10pm, from €20, Tram 13, 17 Westermarkt

37 The romantic Art Deco/Art Nouveau decor alone is reason enough to visit restaurant **De Belhamel,** but the unique menu is a temptation as well. It includes, for example, French toast with *foie gras* and apple, and baked gnocchi with diced eggplant, tomatoes, and spring onions. The terrace, located at the intersection of the Herengracht and Brouwersgracht, is one of the most beautiful spots in Amsterdam.

Brouwersgracht 60, www.belhamel.nl, tel. 020-6221095, open for lunch daily noon-6pm, dinner Sun-Thur 6pm-10pm, Fri-Sat 6pm-10:30pm, from €24.50, Tram 2, 4, 11, 12, 13, 14, 17, 24, 26 Centraal Station, Metro 51, 52, 53, 54 Centraal Station

SHOPPING

1 **The Gift Lab** is a store full of must-haves for anyone who loves to shop. Whether you're looking for home accessories, a beautiful item of clothing, or jewelry, you can choose from a large selection of sustainable and fair-trade brands. This bright and beautiful shop on Haarlemmerstraat also has perfect presents for baby showers. What about a baby coat made from old blankets? Come here to shop for some original gifts.

Haarlemmerstraat 38, www.giftlab.nl, tel. 020-3627737, open Sun noon-6pm, Mon 11am-6pm, Tue-Sat 10am-6pm, Tram 2, 4, 11, 12, 13, 14, 17, 24, 26 Centraal Station, Metro 51, 52, 53, 54 Centraal Station

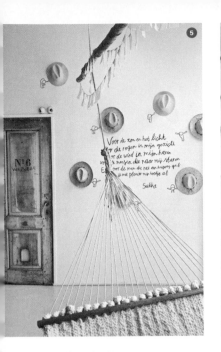

❺ Sukha means "joy" in Sanskrit, and that's exactly what the owners of this eco-friendly store want to create. Handwritten poems and doodles to make you smile hang from the walls. The common thread here is love and attention, from the special home accessories to sustainable clothing and books. Sukha also has its own label with artisan products from India, Nepal, Peru, and Indonesia.
Haarlemmerstraat 110, www.sukha-amsterdam.nl, open Mon 11am-6.30pm, Tue-Sat 10am-6.30pm, Sun noon-5pm, Tram 2, 4, 11, 12, 13, 14, 17, 24, 26 Centraal Station, Metro 51, 52, 53, 54 Centraal Station

❻ If you're in search of something special for your home, **Store Without a Home** is a must. The owner is always on the lookout for furniture, lighting, and home accessories that are otherwise virtually impossible to find in the Netherlands. The collection consists of international interior design from both established and new designers, such as cupboards by Seletti, porcelain by Lenneke Wispelwey, and lamps by Fraumaier.
Haarlemmerdijk 26, www.storewithoutahome.nl, open Mon 1pm-6pm, Tue-Sat 10am-6pm, Tram 3 Haarlemmerplein

❼ In this shop, less is more and "simple" is key to everything they sell. **Restored** has a stunning assortment of minimalist bags, jewelry, clothing, and ceramics, mostly from young designers and niche brands. Some of the items are even one of a kind. The shop itself is a sight to see, with attention paid to the smallest detail. Make sure to check out the beautiful Art Deco details on the storefront before you leave.
Haarlemmerdijk 39, www.restored.nl, tel. 020-3376473, open Sun 1pm-5pm, Mon 1pm-6pm, Tue-Sat 11am-6pm, Tram 3 Haarlemmerplein

✸ At **Het Oud-Hollandsch Snoepwinkeltje** (The Old Dutch Sweet Shop) you can purchase sweets your grandmother might have bought, individually and wrapped in a paper bag. Among the traditional Dutch sweets are ones with enchanting names such as *toverballen* (magic balls) or *duimdrop* (salty licorice). 2e Egelantierdwarsstraat 2, www.snoepwinkeltje.com, tel. 020-4207390, open Tue-Sat 11am-6:30pm, Tram 3, 10 Marnixplein, Tram 13, 17 Westermarkt

⓲ Universe on a T-shirt prints its own designs on its T-shirts and tops. The T-shirts are not only humorous, they are above all original. Plus they feel good because everything is made from organic cotton and guaranteed to be sweatshop-free. Feeling inspired? Then why not buy your own DIY T-shirt box to liven up your old T-shirts. If you can't get enough, there's also a shop on the Bloemstraat.

Nieuwe Leliestraat 6, www.universeonatshirt.com, open daily 11am-6pm, Tram 13, 17 Westermarkt

㉓ You'll find no mild cheese geared at tourists at **De Kaaskamer van Amsterdam**—here you can buy cheeses soaked in *calvados* (a French apple brandy), wrapped in grape leaves, or a simpler mature cheese. This strong-smelling shop not only sells an incredible selection of local produce, but also stocks cheeses from out-of-the-way French mountain areas and small Italian islands. There are also nuts and tasty sausages to complete your picnic basket.

Runstraat 7, www.kaaskamer.nl, tel. 020-6233483, open Mon noon-6pm, Tue-Fri 9am-6pm, Sat 9am-5pm, Sun noon-5:30pm, Tram 2, 11, 12 Spui

㉔ The fragrance and atmosphere of the beautiful **Chocolaterie Pompadour** are enough to make your mouth water as you enter. But perhaps the proprietors also want to teach visitors a thing or two about style—here, craftsmanship is king and the ingredients are as pure as possible. Take note of the paneling, which was created in 1795 for the town hall of Mortsel (Belgium) and has now been given a second life at Pompadour.

Huidenstraat 12, www.pompadour-amsterdam.nl, tel. 020-6239554, open Mon-Fri 10am-6pm, Sat 9am-6pm, Sun noon-6pm, pastry €3.80, eat in €5.25, Tram 2, 11, 12 Spui

㉕ We Are Labels sells things by small, exclusive brands. The team travels all over Europe in search of suppliers. You'll find a selection of 30 exciting brands such as Eleven Paris, Nümph, and Mina UK and accessories by Club Manhattan. We Are Labels has another shop in Huidenstraat and two in Utrechtsestraat.

Hoek Huidenstraat/Herengracht 356, www.welikefashion.com, open Mon noon-6:30pm, Tue-Fri 10:3am0-6:30pm, Sat 10am-6pm, Sun noon-6pm, Tram 2, 11, 12 Spui

30 **meCHICas,** run by owner Debbie, conjures up images of Mexico, color, and passion. The jewelry is handmade from natural materials such as shells, fruit stones, and gems. Alongside its own collection, meCHICas also sells silver jewelry by Mexican designers, hand-painted Mexican pottery, and bags.

Gasthuismolensteeg 11, www.mechicas.com, tel. 020-4203092, open Mon-Wed and Fri 11am-6pm, Thur 11am-7:30pm, Sat 11am-6:30pm, Sun 1pm-6pm, Tram 2, 4, 11, 12, 13, 14, 17, 24 Dam

31 This well-stocked record shop is regularly frequented by many internationally renowned DJs. The owners of **Waxwell Records** have collected some 60,000 records with some real gems among them. While the shop specializes in soul and funk, it also sells old-school rap and other genres. If you're looking for something specific, the staff is happy to help.

Gasthuismolensteeg 8, www.waxwell.com, open Mon-Sat noon-7pm, Sun noon-6pm, Tram 2, 4, 11, 12, 13, 14, 17, 24 Dam

MORE TO EXPLORE

9 The oldest cinema in Amsterdam is not, as you might expect, the Tuschinski, but rather **The Movies.** This stylish cinema, dating from 1912, not only has a beautiful Art Deco interior, but the chairs are also comfortable. It generally shows more unusual art house films.

Haarlemmerdijk 161-163, www.themovies.nl, restaurant open daily from 5:30pm, last film showing usually around 7:45pm, entrance €11, Tram 3 Haarlemmerplein

12 Visit one of the Jordaan's markets for a real taste of this neighborhood's atmosphere. Every Monday, the **Noordermarkt**'s flea market attracts vintage hunters from miles around. You can find some real gems going for a song between the mountains of clothes and shoes. There are also more than enough knickknacks for everyone. On Saturdays, there's an organic farmers' market.

Noordermarkt, www.noordermarkt-amsterdam.nl, open Mon flea market 9am-2pm, Sat farmers' market 9am-4pm, Tram 3 Nieuwe Willemsstraat

14 The Jordaan is known for its many courtyards. You need only know where to find them, as they are often hidden behind a nondescript door or gate. The **Karthuizerhofje** (1650) was originally built for poor widows, but today the houses are rented out to individuals by a housing association. Take a look behind one of those doors and step into another world—a green oasis of tranquility.

Karthuizersstraat 89-171, tram 13, 17 Westermarkt

26 Entering **Proeflokaal de Admiraal** (Admiral's Tasting Room), located in a former coaching inn, is like stepping back into the Netherlands' Golden Age. Sample from among 60 types of liqueur and 16 gins, all artisanally produced according to original recipes. Take a good look around if you visit the restroom—it's constructed in a 10,000-liter oak barrel.

Herengracht 319, www.proeflokaaldeadmiraal.nl, tel. 020-6254334, open Mon-Fri 4:30pm-midnight, Sat 5pm-midnight, Tram 2, 11, 12 Spui

OUD-WEST &
VONDELPARK

ABOUT THE WALK

This walk is for culture lovers who enjoy visiting museums. Museumplein is, of course, not to be missed. You'll also see a lot of interesting architecture, both modern and historical. And the walk also caters to those who like to eat well—there are numerous cafés and restaurants on the Overtoom and in the new Hallen. It's a long walk that can also easily be done by bike.

THE NEIGHBORHOODS

If Amsterdam's elite are to be found anywhere, it's here. And you can't blame them—this is considered one of the best areas of the city, with Amsterdam's most exclusive shopping street (**P. C. Hooftstraat**) and a variety of townhouses, stately mansions, and fine cafés all just around the corner, and the **Vondelpark** as its backyard.

Bordering the Vondelpark, the museum district also offers a significant selection of Amsterdam's most important cultural attractions, such as the **Concertgebouw** (Concert Hall) and the city's three largest museums: the **Rijksmuseum,** the **Stedelijk Museum,** and the **Van Gogh Museum,** which have all been significantly renovated in recent years. The Rijksmuseum reopened its doors in 2013 after a 10-year renovation and is now more impressive than ever. It opens almost directly onto **Museumplein,** and you can once again cycle underneath its grand arch.

Oud-West is characterized by its innumerable, lovely neighborhood cafés and shops. As a result, it has become really popular among young people in their 20s and 30s. On the Overtoom, you'll come across many students and young people who have pulled up a chair for a quick, reasonably priced snack.

An important new hotspot in Oud-West lies in the **Kinkerbuurt** (Kinkerstraat neighborhood). There is new life where Amsterdam's first electrical trams were serviced. The tram depot was built in the early 20th century and since 2014 has been open to the public as **de Hallen**—a center for media, culture, catering, and crafts. It's a great place to eat, drink, or go to the cinema, and interesting events are organized there monthly.

SHORT ON TIME? HERE ARE THE HIGHLIGHTS:

1 RIJKSMUSEUM + 4 VONDELPARK + 16 DE HALLEN + 23 BELLAMYSTRAAT + 36 STEDELIJK MUSEUM

TIPS

// Perfect for culture lovers
// Great during the week if you plan to visit a museum
// You can also follow this route by bike

OUD-WEST & VONDELPARK

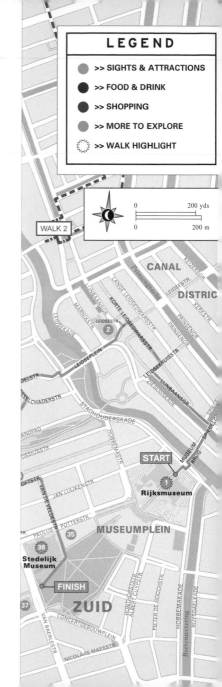

LEGEND

>> SIGHTS & ATTRACTIONS

>> FOOD & DRINK

>> SHOPPING

>> MORE TO EXPLORE

>> WALK HIGHLIGHT

WALK 3 DESCRIPTION (approx. 7 mi/11.5 km)

Start with the Dutch Masters ✹1✹. Walk to Stadhouderskade, cross the bridge and turn left onto Lijnbaansgracht. Keep right and continue on Korte Leidsedwarsstraat to Leidseplein ②. Walk past the Stadsschouwburg theater, cross two streets and turn onto Vondelstraat. Take the first left and the next right past the Zevenlandenhuizen ③. Continue to Vondelpark ✹4✹ ❺ ❻ ❼. Exit the park via Vondelstraat and turn right at the church ❽ in the direction of Overtoom ❾. Cross the street and walk down Tweede Constantijn Huygensstraat. Take the first right, then the first left for coffee ❿ ⓫ and a nice shop ⓬. Continue walking for Asian street food ⓭. Go back and turn left onto Kinkerstraat for more coffee ⓮. Turn right at Bilderdijkkade, then the first left for Hannie Dankbaarpassage ⓯ ✹16✹. Turn right onto Tollensstraat toward Bellamyplein ⓱. Take a left on Ten Katestraat, turn right twice, take Jan Hanzenstraat and continue to Da Costakade. Turn left for two historical buildings ⓲ and continue to De Clercqstraat. Cross the street and turn left on Bilderdijkstraat, then left again into Bilderdijkpark ⓳. Continue to Bilderdijkkade, turn left, then take a right onto De Clercqstraat ⓴ ㉑ ㉒. Take a left on Tweede Kostverlorenkade. Cross the park to Korte Schimmelstraat and continue right onto Jan Hanzenstraat. Turn left and then right at Bellamystraat ✹23✹ ㉔. Turn right onto Van Effenstraat, turn right at the end and then left on Jan Pieter Heijestraat ㉕ ㉖ ㉗. Cross the bridge and turn left, then right on Nicolaas Beetsstraat. Take a left on Arie Biemondstraat to view art installations ㉘ on the grounds of an old hospital. Zigzag to Ite Boeremastraat, turn right, then take a left onto Kanaalstraat. At Jan Pieter Heijestraat turn left ㉙ ㉚. Turn right on Eerste Helmersstraat and continue until you reach Rhijnvis Feithstraat for a pizza with the locals ㉛. Take a left and right onto Overtoom. Cross the street and follow Frederiksstraat to enter Vondelpark. Exit the park at Van Eeghenstraat, turn left on Cornelis Schuytstraat ㉜ and left again on Valeriusstraat. Turn left at the end on Van Breestraat ㉝. At the end of the street, turn left. Continue until you reach Van Eeghenstraat, turn right, then take a left onto Van Baerlestraat. Cross the street and take the second street to the right: P. C. Hooftstraat ㉞. Turn right onto Van de Veldestraat, which ends in front of two of the city's most famous museums ㉟ ✹36✹ and the Concertgebouw ㊲.

SIGHTS & ATTRACTIONS

1 After a thorough renovation, the **Rijksmuseum** reopened in 2013. On display are 8,000 objects in 80 magnificent rooms, spanning 800 years of Dutch art and history. Highlights include Rembrandt's *The Night Watch* and Vermeer's *The Milk Maid*. Make a detour on your way out through the museum's beautiful garden.
Museumstraat 1, www.rijksmuseum.nl, open daily 9am-5pm, entrance €17.50, Tram 2, 5, 12 Rijksmuseum

2 The **Stadsschouwburg** offers the chance to see quality theater and dance daily. It's home to the Netherlands' largest repertory theater company, Toneelgroep Amsterdam (TA), which performs on Thursdays. Now catering to an international audience, the Stadsschouwburg also features international theater productions, in particular from Germany and the UK, and provides subtitles in English and other languages as appropriate.
Leidseplein 26, www.ssba.nl, opening hours dependent on performances, see website for programming and prices, Tram 1, 2, 7, 11, 12, 19 Leidseplein

3 Travel through Europe down one street, thanks to Sam van Eeghen who decided (120 years ago) to build the **Zevenlandenhuizen**: seven houses, each in the style of a different European country. You'll recognize Germany (romantic style), France (in the style of a Loire Valley castle), Spain (inspired by Moorish architecture), Italy (reminiscent of a palazzo), Russia (onion dome), the Netherlands (northern Renaissance), and England (Tudor cottage).
Roemer Visscherstraat 20-30, not open to the public, Tram 1, 11 1e Constantijn Huygensstraat, Tram 3 Overtoom

7 Pierre Cuypers, one of Amsterdam's most famous architects, built his dream home in 1877 alongside Vondelpark: **Villa Pierre Cuypers**. It's directly opposite the much-loved Vondelkerk (also one of his designs) and has both neo-Gothic and neo-Renaissance features. There's a very unique tile panel that shows three men and the old-Dutch text: *Jan bedenckt et, Piet volbrengt et, Claesgen laeckt et. Och wat maeckt et* (Jan invents it, Piet accomplishes it, Claes reproaches it, but who cares). Jan is the architect, Piet the builder, and Claes symbolizes the city that opposed Cuypers's plans.
Vondelstraat 75, not open to the public, Tram 1, 11 1e Constantijn Huygensstraat, Tram 3 Overtoom

⑧ The **Vondelkerk** is an attractive neo-Gothic listed building near the Vondelpark. The church was built in 1872 to a design by Pierre Cuypers, who also designed Centraal Station and the Rijksmuseum. On weekends, the church's main hall can be rented for parties and other gatherings.
Vondelstraat 120d, not open to the public, Tram 1, 11 1e Constantijn Huygensstraat, Tram 3 Overtoom

⑱ Once, there was a brewery on almost every street corner in Amsterdam. The building at number 102 with its red-brick façade recalls those times. It also once served as a wine warehouse. It was designed in 1903 in an eclectic style, with influences from both Neo-Renaissance and Art Nouveau. The tasting rooms were located in the attic. Today it is home to **De Nieuwe Liefde,** a cultural center for public debates, spiritual reflection, and poetry events.
Da Costakade 102-106, www.denieuweliefde.com, opening hours dependent on events, see website for programming and prices, Tram 3 de Clerqstraat 13, 19 Bilderdijkstraat

㉟ There is nowhere else in the world where you can see so many works by artist Vincent Van Gogh in one place. More than 200 paintings are on display at the **Van Gogh Museum,** including *The Potato Eaters*, 500 drawings, 700 letters, and a collection of Japanese prints. Besides works by Van Gogh, there is also a collection of 19th century Post-Impressionist art.
Paulus Potterstraat 7, www.vangoghmuseum.nl, open daily from 9am, see the website for current closing times, entrance €18, Tram 2, 3, 5, 12 Van Baerlestraat

㊱ The **Stedelijk Museum** has undergone years of renovation. Now completed, perhaps the most striking feature is the new wing that, thanks to its shape, is now popularly referred to as the bathtub. In the old building you can view highlights from the museum's large contemporary art collection, while the new section houses temporary exhibitions.
Museumplein 10, www.stedelijk.nl, open Fri-Wed 10am-6pm Thur 10am-10pm, entrance €15, Tram 2, 3, 5, 12 Van Baerlestraat, Tram 24 Museumplein

FOOD & DRINK

5 This unique round building that dates back to 1937 is located smack in the middle of Vondelpark. **'t Blauwe Theehuis** is a relaxed place to have a drink or something to eat. It has an enormous outside terrace where you can always find a spot to relax on a sunny day. On warm summer evenings there are movie nights or free yoga classes, and occasionally there's a party.

Vondelpark 5, www.blauwetheehuis.nl, tel. 020-6620254, open Mon-Fri 9am-6pm, Sat-Sun 9am-7pm, coffee and cake €6.50, Tram 2, 3, 5, 12, Van Baerlestraat

6 After a thorough renovation, the Vondelpark's former pavilion now houses restaurant **Vondelpark/3** and a number of cultural foundations. The restaurant offers Mediterranean-style lunch and dinner with a modern twist. You can also breakfast in style in the stately dining room or have a coffee outside on one of the two large terraces.

Vondelpark 3, www.vondelpark3.nl, tel. 020-6392589, open Sun 10am-8pm, Mon-Tue 10am-6pm, Wed-Sat 10am-midnight, from €14, Tram 1, 11 1e Constantijn Huygensstraat, Tram 3 Overtoom

10 De Koffie Salon is worth a visit not only for the coffee (a few years ago nominated the best in the Netherlands) but also for its location in a beautiful Art Deco building from 1933. Admire the colorful stained-glass windows and geometric designs or enjoy the pleasant terrace outside.

Eerste Constantijn Huygenstraat 82, www.dekoffiesalon.nl, tel. 020-6124079, open daily 7am-7pm, coffee from €2.40, Tram 3 Overtoom

11 Leonie does what many can only dream of—in 2013, she succeeded in making a living baking cakes. At **Baksels** (Bakes), the cakes are simple but tasty. Take a piece of cake to go, or tuck in on a cozy window seat. Leonie's favorite is the raspberry cheesecake brownie.

Bilderdijkstraat 201, www.baksels.nl, tel. 020-3892001, open Tue-Fri 10am-6pm, Sat 11am-5pm, piece of cake €3.50, Tram 3, Kinkerstraat, Tram 7, 17 Bilderdijkstraat

⑬ At **Happyhappyjoyjoy** you'll feel like you've been transported to an Asian street food market with sizzling pans, tantalizing scents, mesmerizing prints, and vibrant colors. It's hard not to feel happy when you're here! The menu features an array of small Asian dishes, all meant for sharing. Choose from a variety of dim sum, noodles, and curries. Pair your meal with a cup of tea or an Asian beer.
Bilderdijkstraat 158, www.happyhappyjoyjoy.asia/en, tel. 020-3446433, open Sun-Thur noon-1am, Fri-Sat noon-2am, dim sum starting at €6.25, tram 3 kinkerstraat, tram 7, 17 bilderdijkstraat

⑭ Step inside **Lot Sixty One Coffee Roasters** for a coffee to go. Speed, however, is not a priority here—the barista likes to create a moment of tranquility around every cup and enjoys involving you in the process. Drop by on a Monday or Tuesday if you can, because that's when the coffee roaster's working—a delight to the senses!
Kinkerstraat 112, www.lotsixtyonecoffee.com, open Mon-Fri 8am-5pm, Sat 9am-5pm, Sun 10am-5pm, coffee from €2, Tram 3 Kinkerstraat, Tram 7, 17 Bilderdijkstraat

17 What better way to start the day than with a delicious Parisian- or New York-style breakfast? **The Breakfast Club** is located on the corner just across from the massively popular Hallen. Come here to indulge in a stack of pancakes with fresh fruit, overnight oats, or eggs made however you like them, with salmon, avocado, or bacon. Wash it all down with a good cup of coffee or a fresh smoothie and you'll be ready to take on the world.

Bellamystraat 2-h, https://thebreakfastclub.nl, tel. 020-2234933, open Mon-Fri 8am-4pm, Sat-Sun 8am-5pm, breakfast starting at €7.50, Tram 7, 17 Ten Katestraat

19 Mexico meets California in Amsterdam! At **Flora,** hidden inside the small and charming Bilderdijkpark, are the best tacos. The small wraps come with a variety of surprising fillings. Try the vegan tacos with black beans and cashew crema or roasted cauliflower with sliced radish, pomegranate seeds, and zesty lime sauce. The cocktails are delightful as well, and on a summer's night this is a great place to relax and enjoy an entire evening.

Bilderdijkpark 1a, open Sat-Sun noon-11pm, Wed-Fri 6pm-11pm, three courses €25, Tram 3 De Clercqstraat, 13, 19 Bilderdijkstraat

20 There's nothing clichéd about Greek restaurant **To Ouzeri,** from its blue awning to its bright decor, surprising menu, and fresh food. Try the *mezedes*, Greek tapas that can easily match the more famous Spanish variation. What about *tiri saganaki*—mature, melted cheese flambéed with Greek brandy? The *kolokithokeftedes* is also worth a try, provided, of course, you can pronounce it!

De Clercqstraat 106, www.toouzeri.nl, tel. 020-6181412, open Wed-Sun 5pm–11pm, from €7, Tram 3 De Clerqstraat, Tram 13, 19 Bilderdijkstraat

22 If you enter this authentic pub, it's hard to believe it opened only about ten years ago. **Café Thuys** is a bit like the Kinkerbuurt's local, where everyone joins in the pub quiz, watches soccer, and orders an affordable dish of the day (ranging from schnitzels to casserole). The terrace opens as soon as the sun shines. The view from the pub is never boring, with all the activity on the water and the passing traffic.

De Clercqstraat 129, www.cafe-thuys.nl, tel. 020-6120898, open Sun-Thur 11am-1pm, Fri-Sat 11am-2pm, from €15, Tram 13, 19 Willem De Zwijgerlaan

㉗ Deegrollers (Dough Rollers) is a pizzeria with a traditional Dutch name but real Italian pizza made by an Italian chef. You can taste it too—in the thin crust, fresh ingredients, and the truly Italian combinations, such as truffle with pecorino, and pancetta with mushrooms. Traditional pizzas like Margherita and *cinque formaggi* have not, however, been omitted from the menu. For an original Italian atmosphere eat inside at long, wooden tables or in good weather sit outside overlooking the canal.
Jan Pieter Heijestraat 110, tel. 020-2212098, open daily 5pm-10pm, pizza €13, Tram 1, 7, 11, 17 J. P. Heijestraat

㉙ Soup with meatballs—it sounds Dutch, but **Voldaan** proves this combination can be created in any cuisine. There's a delicious Arabic version of lentil soup with spicy lamb meatballs. There's always a vegetarian and a gluten-free option on the menu, too, and the delicious dips, chutneys, and compotes are for sale in storage jars, so you can reminisce at home.
Jan Pieter Heijestraat 121, open Tue-Sun noon-8:30pm, from €7.95, Tram 1, 7, 11, 17 J. P. Heijestraat

㉛ Forno's pizzas are among the most popular in Oud-West, keeping this trendy restaurant's *pizzaiolos* constantly busy. The idea is simple: straightforward decor, a large terrace, and pizzas straight from the wood oven. And that's not all, Forno's has good antipasti (oysters and roasted beetroot, for example), unusual toppings (what about pizza calzone with venison?), and high-quality wines and proseccos.
Rhijnvis Feithstraat 43, tel. 020-6187415, open daily 11am-1pm, pizza €13, Tram 1, 11 Rhijnvis Feithstraat

㉜ The Bertram family opened its first bakery in 1890 in the Amsterdam neighborhood Jordaan. Nowadays **Bakker Bertram** is located on the corner of the lively Cornelis Schuytstraat. Enjoy your freshly made sandwich and coffee out front or find a table inside this cozy neighborhood store. Everything you see is baked on the premises. And for early birds the doors open at 7:30 am. It's a great place to pop by on a morning walk through Vondelpark.
Cornelis Schuytstraat 34, www.bakkerbertram-amsterdam.nl, tel. 020-3319042, open Sun 8:30am-4pm, Mon-Fri 7:30am-5pm, Sat 8am-5pm, coffee starting at €2, Tram 2 Cornelis Schuytstraat

SHOPPING

9 Amsterdammers who love to travel know that **Pied à Terre** is the largest travel bookstore in Amsterdam. The shop has a huge collection of travel guides, globes, hiking maps, and much more for anyone with any interest in travel.
Overtoom 135-137, www.piedaterre.nl, tel. 020-6274455, open Mon 1pm-6pm, Tue-Wed & Fri 10am-6pm, Thur 10am-9pm, Sat 10am-5pm, Tram 1, 11 1e Constantijn Huygensstraat

12 Sisters **Jutka & Riska** sell vintage clothing—their own designs and creations by young designers—here and at three other locations in Amsterdam, Antwerp, and Haarlem. Conveniently sorted by color and constantly changing, the store's unique garments are also a great value. The collection includes a wide range of bags, jewelry, sunglasses, and shoes.
Bilderdijkstraat 194, www.jutkaenriska.nl, tel. 020-6188021, open Fri-Wed 10:30am-7pm, Thur 10:30am-9pm, Tram 3 Kinkerstraat, Tram 7, 17 Bilderdijkstraat

⑮ Stop in **The Gathershop** for handmade jewelry and other beautiful fair-trade items—all with a story to tell and many by boutique designer studios. Magazines, succulents, skincare supplies, and stationery—each item is as beautiful as the next. The white space has a minimalist décor, and it's the perfect place to pick up a present for someone or for you. The shop is located in the "Kleine Hallen," a passage with a number of different stores.

Hannie Dankbaarpassage 19, www.gathershop.nl, open Sun & Tue-Sat noon-6pm, Tram 7, 17 Ten Katestraat

㉑ If office supplies conjure images of boring paper clips, staplers, and binders, then you've never been to **Misc Store.** The online store was a huge success, with its stationery to make you smile. Now the wonderful (traveler's) notebooks, calendars, and pens can be admired in a showroom. Your desk will never look the same again!

De Clerqstraat 130, www.misc-store.com, tel. 020-7009855, open Tue-Fri 11am-6.30pm, Sat 10am-6pm, Tram 13, 19 Willem De Zwijgerlaan

㉔ The founders of the **Creative Garage** refer to their initiative as a "drop-off shop." It's a platform for twenty artists who make unique products but can't afford to open their own store. There's a special selection of handmade bags, jewelry, clothes, and home accessories—ideal gifts for a great price. Both adults and children are welcome for workshops and other activities, and also just for a drink.

Bellamystraat 91, decreatievegarage.wordpress.com, tel. 061-9979967, open Tue-Sat 11am-5pm, Tram 7, 17 Ten Katestraat

㉕ **Bullitt**'s amicable owners are incredibly enthusiastic about design, art, styling, and fashion, something they have managed to transmit through their store. They don't limit themselves to a particular style but rather stock what they find attractive themselves, whether clothing or accessories, homemade jewelry, or vintage hi-fi, lighting, or glassware.

Jan Pieter Heijestraat 91-93, www.bullittamsterdam.nl, tel. 020-6180007, open Tue-Fri 11am-6.30pm, Sat 11am-6pm, Tram 7, 17 J. P. Heijestraat

㉖ At **Frankie's Corner,** *kwarkbollen* (quark balls, similar to scones) are made with farm-produced quark and cranberries, organic corn bread with pumpkin, or whole wheat bread with walnuts. Every week, baker Frank introduces new creations that are healthy, organic, and preservative-free. And as befits any real corner store owner, he knows exactly what's happening in the neighborhood and is always up for a chat.

Jan Pieter Heijestraat 95, tel. 020-6121776, open Mon-Sat 7am-6pm, Tram 1, 11 J. P. Heijestraat

㉚ This slick store that sells athletic shoes, demonstrates that sneakers can be as desirable as high heels. The impressive collection has been inspired by London's love of the athletic shoe. Brands such as Supra, Creative Recreation, Goliath Shabbies, and Radical are stylish, different, and striking—precisely the vibe that **Label 1401** aims to create.

Jan Pieter Heijestraat 153, https://label1401.com, tel. 020-6161734, open Tue-Wed & Fri 10am-6pm, Thur 10am-8pm, Sat 10am-5pm, Tram 1, 11 J.P. Heijestraat

㉝ **&klevering** sells original home accessories and gifts by its own label &K amsterdam, together with other leading brands such as HAY, littala, and firm LIVING. From cabinets to cushions and from lamps to toys, all items are equally fun. There is also a secondhand store in the Jordaan on Haarlemmerstraat.

Jacob Obrechtstraat 19a, www.klevering.nl, tel. 020-6703623, open Mon noon-6:30, Tue-Fri 10:30am-6:30pm, Sat 10am-6pm, Sun 11:30am-6pm, Tram 2 Cornelis Schuytstraat

MORE TO EXPLORE

④ For many Amsterdammers, the **Vondelpark** is their garden. It's the ideal place for romantic picnics or family celebrations with a party tent and a barbecue. In summer, the Openluchttheater (open-air theater) also offers free dance, drama, and musical performances, from Wednesday to Sunday.

Constantijn Huygenstraat, www.hetvondelpark.net, open daily, Tram 2, 3, 5, 12, Van Baerlestraat

In the late 19th century, **De Hallen** was the largest tram depot in the city. The large complex has recently been developed into a location for creative enterprises, with several TV studios, a cinema with an Art Deco room, a library with a literary café, restaurants, and an industrial hotel. In addition, there's the monthly Local Goods Weekend Market with products from Amsterdam.

Hannie Dankbaar Passage 33, www.dehallen-amsterdam.nl, tel. 020-7058164, open Sun-Thur 7am-1am, Fri-Sat 7am-3am, Tram 7, 17 Ten Katestraat

Entering this charming street is like taking a step back in time. The **Bellamystraat** is still at the old, lower polder level of all the villages around Amsterdam before the city's expansion in 1865. Now the street stands out among the "new" buildings from the second half of the 19th century.

Bellamystraat, Tram 7, 17 Ten Katestraat

㉘ **Lab111** is hidden away in a former anatomical pathology lab in the Wilhelmina Gasthuis complex. Enjoy excellent food, watch movies you won't see anywhere else, check out various art projects, and enjoy experimental music.

Arie Biemondstraat 101-111, www.lab111.nl, tel. 020-6169994, open Mon-Thur noon-1am, Fri noon-3pm, Sat 2pm-3am, Sun 2pm-1am, movie tickets €9, mains from €15, dinner and movie €20, Tram 7, 17 Ten Katestraat

㉞ Celebrities, expensive cars, and tourists jostle on **P. C. Hooftstraat** where it's all about seeing and being seen. The street boasts some of the chicest brands. If "the PC" is somewhat beyond your budget, then it's the perfect place to just sit and people watch.

P. C. Hooftstraat, www.pchooftstraat.nl, Tram 2, 3, 5, 12 Van Baerlestraat

㊲ The **Concertgebouw** is one of the most popular classical concert halls in the world, renowned for its perfect acoustics. If you'd like to attend a concert, it's best to book well in advance. Or go to one of the free performances held every Wednesday 12:30-1pm (arrive early)!

Concertgebouwplein 10, www.concertgebouw.nl, tel. 090-06718345, see website for program and prices, Tram 3, 5, 12, 24 Museumplein

WEST & WESTERPARK

ABOUT THE WALK

If you're interested in going for a stroll through a colorful neighborhood with many creative initiatives, then this walk is for you. Discover interesting shops and small cafés on Jan Evertsenstraat and enjoy the greenery as you walk through Erasmuspark and Westerpark. If you want to know more about the interesting Amsterdam School architectural style, don't miss a guided tour of Museum Het Schip. From Centraal Station, take tram 13 to Admiraal de Ruijterweg, where the walk starts.

THE NEIGHBORHOODS

De Baarsjes and **Bos en Lommer**: until a few years ago, these were neighborhoods Amsterdammers avoided. Their dubious reputation means they're hardly mentioned in any city guide. It's a shame because these are some of the most exciting, up-and-coming areas of Amsterdam. Local businesses and residents took it upon themselves to make improvements to their neighborhoods. Initiatives such as "Geef om de Jan Eef" (Care about **Jan Evertsenstraat** shopping street) and BoLo Boost (Boost Bos en Lommer) have brought new life into impoverished streets and neighborhoods. Now they're bubbling with pop-up stores and weekend markets, making the area great for shopping. You may not find any big chain stores here, but there is more space for small entrepreneurs with unique ideas.

West Amsterdam is still very much alive and kicking and is characterized by multicultural diversity and many creative enterprises. **Westergasterrein** in the **Westerpark** is an important hub for this creative scene. Many years have passed since its factories supplied the city with gas. Today the buildings that used to house transformers and machines are home to cafés, a cinema, and creative businesses. During the summer, the Westerpark is a venue for weekend festivals, and once a month there's the Sunday Market.

It's nothing new that Amsterdam West is a focal point for creative energy. Around 100 years ago, architects from the Amsterdam School gave free rein to their imagination. The result is the **Spaarndammerbuurt,** where you'll find an incredible concentration of buildings in this style.

SHORT ON TIME? HERE ARE THE HIGHLIGHTS:

8 BAR BAARSCH + 17 PIZZAS AT BUURMAN & BUURMAN + 25 WESTERPARK + 27 WESTERGASTERREIN + 34 MUSEUM HET SCHIP

TIPS

// An interesting walk off the beaten path
// Ideal for weekends because of the activities in the park
// You can follow this route by bike

WEST & WESTERPARK

WALK 4 DESCRIPTION (approx. 7.5 mi/12 km)

Start on Admiraal de Ruijterweg **1** **2** **3**, which turns into Jan Evertsenstraat, the beating heart of trendy Amsterdam West **4** **5** **6** **7** **8** **9** **10** **11**. Take a tour of the special architecture on Mercatorplein **12**, walk under the arch to Mercatorstraat, turn right onto Jan Maijenstraat and continue to the Jeruzalemkerk **13**. Turn right onto James Cookstraat, then turn left twice to reach the green Vespuccistraat **14**. Continue to Erasmuspark **15**. Take the first left **16**. Cross the water on the right and walk down Mercatorstraat **17**. Continue for a while alongside the water until you reach Hoofdweg. Turn right over the bridge and walk to the left to Wilde Westen **18**, or immediately turn right alongside the water. Turn left onto Griseldestraat and continue until you reach Tijl Uilenspiegelstraat. Turn left. Via the little street on the right and the stairs you'll reach Bos en Lommerweg. Cross the road and turn onto Gulden Winckelplantsoen: now you're in Bosleeuw Midden **19**. Turn right onto Leeuwendalersweg and check out the so-called piggelmee-houses, then turn right onto Hofwijckstraat to return to Bos en Lommerweg, where you turn left **20** **21** **22**. Follow the street until you reach Willem de Zwijgerlaan. Turn right and left onto Adolf van Nassaustraat for some tasty pickles **23**. Continue on to Nieuwpoortstraat and turn right. Head left on Nieuwpoortkade, walk past the windmill **24**, and turn right onto Haarlemmerweg. Continue until you can turn left over the water to head to the Westerpark **25**. Turn right and pass by Mossel & Gin **26** onto the Westergasterrein **27** **28** **29**. Head left in the direction of the railway and turn right, following the railway until the second tunnel. Go through the tunnel to reach the Spaarndammerstraat **30**. Turn left for a short diversion to Hammam **31**, or continue to two special restaurants **32** **33**. Turn left onto Knollendamstraat and walk clockwise around the Spaarndammerplantsoen to view one of the highlights of the Amsterdam School architectural style **34**. Walk via Oostzaanstraat to Hembrugstraat, turn right and walk to the water. Continue to Houthavens **35** to **36** **37** or take a right onto Stettineiland that becomes Memeleiland. Walk until you can't go any farther. Take a right and the first left toward Tasmanstraat, follow this street, cross the water and through Van Diemenstraat to end at Bak Restaurant **38**.

SIGHTS & ATTRACTIONS

12 Designed by the famous Dutch architect H. P. Berlage, **Mercatorplein** was destined to become the focal point of Amsterdam West in the mid-1920s. But its cafés, theater, cinema, and department store never materialized, and the square took on a purely residential and business function. It wasn't cheap to live here, so at first it attracted mainly affluent newcomers. By the 1980s, however, the area had fallen into disrepair and had earned a bad reputation. It has since gone through two renovations—in 1998 and again in 2008—that have breathed new life into the square and its surroundings.

Mercatorplein, Tram 7, 13 Mercatorplein

13 Amsterdam West is a magnet for lovers of the Amsterdam School, an architectural style that developed in the Netherlands between 1910 and 1930. The **Jeruzalemkerk** (Jerusalem Church) is without doubt one of the finest buildings constructed in that style (1928-1929). The architect deliberately designed the church so it would be attached to housing, to express God's desire to live among the people. The symmetry of the façade and the fact that the church is oriented north-south, rather than the usual east-west, is striking. The seven stained-glass windows symbolize the seven days of creation.

Jan Maijenstraat 14, www.jeruzalem-kerk.nl, Tram 7, 13 Mercatorplein

14 The **Vespuccistraat** is a good example of how the neighborhood has taken matters into its own hands. Nearly one hundred years ago, the street was designed as a green avenue leading to the Erasmus Park, with front gardens, rare trees, and houses in Amsterdam School style. Over recent years, half of the gardens were lovingly maintained by the residents, with the other half left in the uninspired hands of the municipality. Then, residents decided the gardens should be restored to their 1920s appeal. Fortunately, 40 Japanese ginkgo trees have stood the test of time— they are some of the few that can be found in the Netherlands.

Vespuccistraat, Tram 13, 18 Marco Polostraat

19 **Bosleeuw Midden** now seems to be a typical residential area, but in 1935 it was a revolutionary idea in the context of the "Bosch en Lommer expansion plan." Architect Cornelis van Eesteren worked with open housing blocks, open courtyards, and lush greenery. It was an example of "new construction" in which home, work, and recreation were separated and accommodation was affordable. Behind, on the Leeuwendalersweg,

you'll find the *piggelmeewoningen* ("gnome homes"—Piggelmee is a gnome in an Old Dutch book for children). They're probably the most intimate single-story family homes in the city at 366 square feet (34 square meters)—though not for long, as they're due to be demolished.

Tussen de a10, Admiraal de Ruijterweg, Wiltzanghlaan En Leeuwendalersweg, Tram 7 Bos en Lommerplein

㉔ Molen de Bloem (Flower Mill) might look as though it's been here for centuries, but that's not the case. From 1786 to 1878 it stood in the center of Amsterdam, on the Bloemgracht (Flower Canal), from where it got its name. When the Marnixstraat was laid in the 1870s, the mill had to move. It was rebuilt in 1921 and has since been modernized several times. Flour was still ground here until 1960, but now the mill runs only occasionally.

Haarlemmerweg 465, not open to the public, Tram 19 Bos en Lommerweg

㉕ When the Westergasfabriek was built in 1883, it was the biggest coal and gas plant in the Netherlands. The factory still produced gas until the 1960s. Nowadays, the **Westergasterrein** is a green cultural complex. Spaces are rented to creative, cultural, and innovative entrepreneurs, from restaurants to clubs and galleries to

studios. For partygoers there's Pacific Parc, plus a host of fun festivals taking place throughout the year.
Polonceaukade, www.westergasfabriek.nl, tel. 020-5860710, open daily, Tram 5 Van Hallstraat

Museum Het Schip was built in 1921 as a combination of post office and residences in Amsterdam School style. For several years, it has served as a museum for the Amsterdam School. The property should be seen from the inside—only then does it become clear how the architects intended to reconcile the interior and exterior. The museum house still has an authentic 1920s interior.
Spaarndammerplantsoen 140, www.hetschip.nl, tel. 020-6868595, open Tue-Sun 11am-5pm, entrance €7.50, Tram 3 Haarlemmerplein

The **Houthavens** were dug in 1876 for transshipping and storing wood. It was the first harbor in Amsterdam that was man-made. Nowadays the area is being redeveloped and is set to become a brand-new city district. A 269-foot-high (82-meter-high) building known as Pontsteigergebouw, designed by Arons en Gelauff Architecten, was erected on the former ferry dock at Tasmanstraat. It made headlines at the start of 2016 because the penthouse apartment—which was yet to be built—sold to Amsterdam hospitality entrepreneur Won Yip for 16 million euros.
Houthavenkade, Tram 3 Zoutkeetsgracht, Bus 48, 248 Koivistokade

FOOD & DRINK

Cozy corners, beautiful industrial lamps, and a large sofa—start your day at **Bar Spek** (Bacon Bar) with a latte, tasty tea, or an unusual smoothie, like the green monster or Bloody Mary. Or choose from oysters, tasty pizzas, and other Italian delicacies such as *melanzane alla parmigiana*, and an extensive selection of mouth-watering desserts.
Admiraal de Ruijterweg 1, www.barspek.nl, tel. 020-6188102, open Mon-Thur 8am-1am, Fri-Sat 9am-2am, Sun 9am-1am, pizza €12.50, Tram 12, 13, 14 Willem de Zwijgerlaan

Falafel and beer—that's what **Bar Kauffmann** is all about. And the falafel is unlike any you've tasted before. It's served in pita bread or as a salad, homemade and flavorful. This is the perfect spot for vegetarians and beer lovers alike, with some 30 kinds of craft beer in all. For those in the know, this place is located just off-route on a side street. It also has a small outdoor seating area in the sun, making it a popular summertime hangout.

Reinier Claeszenstraat 4b, barkauffmann.nl, tel. 020-8461606, open Sun-Thur 5pm-11pm, Fri-Sat 5pm-1am, falafel starting at €10.50, Tram 13, 19 Willem de Zwijgerlaan

❺ Radijs (Radish) is proud of its location in the newly spruced-up West district of Amsterdam and features menu items inspired by the neighborhood, including Oude Baarsjes, a sandwich with mini pickles and mustard. You can't get more Amsterdamese! Try a special beer from a local brewery or sample honey from the city beekeeper while enjoying the industrial interior with an extensive use of wood. Or sit outside on the terrace overlooking the water.

Jan Evertsenstraat 41, www.radijs-amsterdam.nl, tel. 020-7513232, open Mon-Fri 8:30am-2am, Sat 10am-2am, Sun 10am-1am, from €16.50, Tram 13, 18 Marco Polostraat

❻ At **Deli-caat** you'll find homemade French bread and quiches, fruit, vegetables, and organic food. Sit down for a cup of coffee by White Label or a sandwich. The owners describe their business as a mix between delicatessen, lunchroom, and coffee bar. They like to talk through your choice with you. Their priority? Everything should be really tasty.

Admiralengracht 223, www.deli-caat.nl, tel. 063-8103649, open Mon, Sat & Sun 4pm-9pm, Tue-Fri 11am–9pm, from €12, Tram 13, 18 Marco Polostraat

❽ With a relentless stream of clientele in this busy location, it would be no exaggeration to call **Bar Baarsch** the focal point of the Baarsjes. Business lunches, Friday afternoon drinks, spontaneous dinners, lively parties, and hearty breakfasts—everything goes here. It's a local pub but with a more contemporary feel, good food, an extensive beer list (many American specialty beers), 30 varieties of whisky, and fresh ginger tea.

Jan Evertsenstraat 91, tel. 020-6181970, open Mon-Thur 10am-1am, Fri 10am-3am, Sat 11am-3am, Sun 11am-1am, from €16.50, Tram 13, 18 Marco Polostraat

❾ Burgers and beer—that's what **Bar Frits** serves. The large outdoor seating area on Mercatorplein is a great place to hang out. This is a friendly neighborhood bar with great character, and the staff is equally cheerful. It's the type of place where you can enjoy a tasty burger (vegetarian options available) and find yourself staying easily until the wee hours of the morning. The beer menu is so extensive, you can try something new from a different part of the world every time you visit.

Jan Evertsenstraat 91, frits-amsterdam.nl, tel. 020-2339796, open Sun-Thur 4pm-1am, Fri & Sat 4pm-3am, burgers start at €9.75, Tram 13, 18 Marco Polostraat

❶ White Label Coffee aims to evoke the raw atmosphere of Brooklyn with its slick, rugged business. The coffee here is freshly roasted and takes center stage, preferably without milk and unaccompanied by plates of cakes. The tea comes from Amsterdam Monkey Chief Tea and chocolate from Chocolatl Amsterdam. Coffee is also sold separately, including all the things you need to prepare that perfect cup of coffee.

Jan Evertsenstraat 136, www.whitelabelcoffee.nl, tel. 020-7371359, open Mon-Fri 8am-6pm, Sat-Sun 9am-6pm, Tram 7, 13 Mercatorplein

❶❻ At Terrasmus, situated in Erasmus Park, you'll find juices, smoothies, and ice creams, perfect for the summer months, when nothing could be better than sitting on the terrace or taking your snack and drink to sit on the grass. During summer, you can also enjoy all kinds of musical activities that are organized in or around the café. In bad weather, take refuge inside with a hot soup or drink, wraps, or a luxury sandwich. Note that the café is closed November-February.

Erasmuspark, www.terrasmus.nl, tel. 020-3343468, open Mar-Oct daily 10am-6pm (sometimes later), toasty €3.75, Tram 7 Jan Van Galenstraat

❶❼ The friendly neighbors who run **Eetwinkel Buurman & Buurman** wanted to breathe new life into this dark corner building. And with the help of friends they succeeded to magically turn it into a local place to cook and eat. The wood-fired oven at its heart is guaranteed to produce the best pizzas. Ingredients for all dishes are sourced locally. You can also buy Amsterdam limoncello, Himalayan salt, and Turkish olive oil.

Mercatorstraat 171, www.eetwinkelbuurmanenbuurman.nl, tel. 020-2628262, open daily 5pm-midnight, from €12, Tram 7 Erasmusgracht

❶❽ Wilde Westen is located in the basement of the old GAK-building (a now defunct government agency) in the Bos & Lommer neighborhood. The interior is industrial, but it has succeeded in creating a living room atmosphere with a hipster vibe where you'll feel right at home. During the day, young creatives come here to work and to eat lunch. In the evening great pizzas are served from a wood-fired oven. On "Cheap Mondays," every pizza on the menu costs €9. Try their pizza Arabica!

Bos en Lommerplantsoen 1 , www.wilde-westen.nl, tel. 020-7608290, open Sun 10am-1am, Mon-Thur 9am-1am, Fri 9am-3am, Sat 10am-3am, mains from €13, Tram 7 Erasmusgracht

22 It's not trendy, and there's no excessive decoration. It's simply an Indonesian restaurant, as was intended. **Betawi** started here more than thirty years ago now. The *nasi rames* is famous, and the vegetarian dishes are also delicious; the aubergine dish is a must.

Admiraal de Ruijterweg 337, www.betawi.nl, tel. 020-6821885, open Tue-Sun 4-10pm, from €10, Tram 19 Bos en Lommerweg

26 **Mossel & Gin** specializes in—you guessed it—mussels and gin and tonics. This fun food bar in the middle of Westerpark knows how to surprise with both taste and presentation. This is not a rustic place where you'll find the classic black pans filled to the brim with mussels. Try the Thai mussels with coconut curry and lime or the Surinamese mussels with peanut sauce and long beans. The homemade signature gin mayo, found on every table, can be purchased by the tube and makes for a great souvenir.

Gosschalklaan 12, www.mosselengin.nl, tel. 020-4865869, open Sat & Sun 1pm-midnight, Tue-Thur 4pm-midnight, Fri 2pm-1am, mussels €16.50, Tram 5 Van Hallstraat

28 Quirky is perhaps the description that best fits rock 'n' roll **Pacific Parc** restaurant. The interior of this large industrial space is nicely messy, while the benches lining the wall are a good place from which to people watch. A cozy fire burns in the winter, and in the summer, you can sit in princely splendor on the terrace. From Thursday to Saturday evenings, the tables are pushed aside to make room for live music and DJs.

Polonceaukade 23, www.pacificparc.nl, tel. 020-4887778, open Mon-Wed 11am-1am, Fri-Sat 11am-3am, Sun 11am-11pm, from €17, Tram 5 Van Limburg Stirumplein

32 "You're crazy if you don't come to eat here," said former mayor Job Cohen at the opening of **Restaurant Freud.** You would be crazy to miss the delicious food as well as the restaurant's special and particularly dedicated staff. The 80 employees have all struggled with mental illness or addiction and are given a special opportunity here. Everything is homemade, right up to the cakes and chocolates. In addition, dishes contain only free-range meat, responsibly caught fish, and, wherever possible, organic vegetables. Your dinner couldn't be more socially responsible!

Spaarndammerstraat 424, www.restaurantfreud.nl, tel. 020-6885548, open Tue-Sun 11am-11pm, from €19.75, Tram 3 Haarlemmerplein

33 First the bad news—from five o'clock in the afternoon, it's only possible to get take-away. Now for the good news—Westerpark is around the corner, and **DopHert** goes all out to give a new dimension to all things vegan. Everything at this lunchroom is completely vegan from lattes made with almond milk, sandwiches with vegan cheese, and meatloaf made from lentils. It even sells vegan accessories, including cosmetics and condoms!
Spaarndammerstraat 49, www.dophertcatering.nl, tel. 020 7520581, open Wed-Fri noon-9pm, Sat 10am-9pm, Sun 11am-5pm, sandwiches €6.50, Tram 3 Haarlemmerplein

36 Father Ad and son Steven are the brains behind the brilliant concept that is **Wilde Kroketten.** Here you eat handmade *kroketten* (traditional Dutch croquettes) with bread and salad. They make the broth that serves as the base themselves, producing the best croquettes imaginable. Choose from some twenty varieties: besides the classic beef croquette, there is Asian duck, spicy Indonesian meat, and lentil and goat cheese croquettes. In the evening a four-course dinner is served, consisting of croquettes and other delicacies.
Danzigerkade 27, wildekroketten.nl, tel. 020-7372909, open Sun & Wed-Sat noon-10pm, Mon & Tue noon-4pm, mains from €16, Bus 48, 248 Koivistokade

37 Once upon a time **REM Eiland** was a platform located 6 miles off the coast of Noordwijk in the North Sea. From here Radio and TV Noordzee broadcast its rebellious pirate radio and television shows. Nowadays this unique building is located in the Houthavens and houses a restaurant with phenomenal views over the Amsterdam harbor. Order the chef's menu and indulge in the pure and fresh ingredients that are used.

Haparandadam 45-2, www.remeiland.com, tel. 020-6885501, open daily noon-10pm, mains from €25, Bus 48, 248 Koivistokade

38 If you love unique ingredients and original combinations, **Restaurant BAK** is the place to be. There are no *à la carte* dishes but instead a tasting menu that changes with the seasons and availability of the ingredients. Let the chef surprise you with fresh heirloom vegetables and other organic—mostly locally sourced—products. Many of the dishes are works of art on a plate, and the wine list boasts a beautiful selection. This is the perfect place for a truly exquisite dining experience.

Van Diemenstraat 408, www.bakrestaurant.nl, tel. 020-7372553, open Sat & Sun 12:30pm-1am, Wed-Fri 7pm-1am, chef's tasting menu €60, Tram 3 Zoutkeetsgracht, Bus 48 Houtmankade

SHOPPING

9 With their knowledge and love of wine, the nice guys behind **The Wine Spot** demonstrate that purchasing wine is far from dull and could even be one of the world's most enjoyable pastimes. They'll happily advise you on the right wine to accompany that dinner dish. The wines are imported from seven European countries, including Romania. Chilled wine and specialty beers can also be purchased here.

Admiraal de Ruijterweg 43, www.thewinespot.nl, tel. 020-7372212, open Mon 2-7pm, Tue-Fri 11am-7pm, Sat 10am-7pm, Sun noon-6pm, Tram 13, 19 Willem de Zwijgerlaan

10 Reap the rewards of Sanne and Petra's choosy collector mania at **Things I Like Things I Love.** Their carefully selected mix of vintage and new clothing, created by prominent designers, also includes knitwear from neighbor Willie. Sanne and Petra also furnish houses, offices, and hotels on request, such as Hotel Dwars.

Jan Evertsenstraat 106, www.thingsilikethingsilove.com, tel. 020-2239254, open Mon-Tue 1-5:30pm, Wed-Sat 11-5:30pm, Sun 1-5pm, Tram 13, 18 Marco Polostraat

20 It was risky to open this bookshop in Bos en Lommer (BoLo), a gritty neighborhood undergoing urban renewal. However, **De Nieuwe Boekhandel** has become a lively meeting point. It's the place to buy BoLo goodies. As befits a bookshop, lectures, book reviews, and workshops are also organized here. Don't forget to check out the Wall of Fame! Owner Monique has her own claim to fame, as book panel member on *De Wereld Draait Door*, a popular Dutch talk show broadcast live from Amsterdam.

Bos en Lommerweg 227, www.libris.nl/denieuweboekhandel, tel. 020-4867722, open Mon 1-6pm, Thur-Fri 10am-6pm, Sat 10am-5pm, Tram 19 Bos en Lommerweg

23 If you're a fan of onions, pickles, and Dutch mustard, chances are those came from **Kesbeke Zoet & Zuur,** supermarket brands included. Today, the 70-year-old business is the sole supplier of Amsterdam pickles. Apart from pickles, it's also the place for special oils and vinegars—indeed, everything you need to pickle fruit and vegetables yourself. Before you know it, you'll have left laden with dragon oil, porcini, and preserving jars.

Adolf Van Nassaustraat 3, www.zoetenzuur.nl, tel. 020-3032650, open Wed-Fri 11am-5pm, Sat 10am-5pm, Tram 19 Bos en Lommerweg

30 **Kweek Stadstuinwinkel** has everything anyone with green fingers but not much space could ever wish for—organic herbs, organic vegetables that can be grown in pots or in a roof garden, small tools, hanging gardens, and mini gardens in boxes. The store sells only organic products, from soil to fertilizers and plant protection.

Spaarndammerstraat 54, www.spaarndammerstraat.nl/winkel/kweek-stadstuinwinkel, tel. 020-3705181, open Tue-Fri 10am-6pm, Sat 10am-5pm, Tram 3 Haarlemmerplein

MORE TO EXPLORE

4 **TOON Amsterdam** is a podium shop that offers creative entrepreneurs, artists, and designers a place to show their work. At TOON you'll find small gifts and exclusive pieces of art. There are cultural events on a regular basis, such as "living room performances," album launches, and book presentations. A visit to this dynamic place is always surprising.

Jan Evertsenstraat 4-6-8, www.toon.amsterdam, tel. 064-2011831, open Tue-Sat 10am-6pm, Sun noon-6pm, Tram 13, 19 Admiraal de Ruijterweg

WELCOME TO OUR
A PLACE WHERE NEW I
MIXED WITH VINTA
SECOND HAND
WHERE
THING
NGS
VE

7 Following a successful crowdfunding campaign **Kattencafé Kopjes** opened its doors in 2015, with no less than 600 cat lovers lined up on the waitlist. The café is home to eight different cats that want for nothing. Here you can enjoy a *catuccino* with a slice of cake or something from the lunch menu. They can accommodate only 20 people at a time, so be sure to make reservations. Patrons pay an additional "cat tax" of 3 euros, used to help keep the cats happy and healthy.
Marco Polostraat 211, kattencafekopjes.nl, tel. 020-7370999, open Wed-Sun 10am-7pm, entrance €3, Tram 13, 18 Marco Polostraat

15 **Erasmus Park** is not just a park—it was laid out where only a hundred years ago there was nothing but polder, complete with meadows and ditches. As a Mondrian painting seeks harmony in surface, color, and line, so the park seeks to create harmony between paths, trees, and grass. There's a rose garden in the middle of the park, and on the side of Jan van Galenstraat you'll find various statues.
Erasmuspark, Tram 7, 19 Jan Van Galenstraat

㉑ The former Pniëlkerk has grown to become the cultural heart of the Bos en Lommer district. **Podium Mozaïek**'s repertoire includes dance, theater, world music, and cabaret. It's also home to a number of studios and workshops. Works by new artists are displayed in the exhibition space, and on weekends between 10am and 3pm you can enjoy a traditional Turkish breakfast in the theater café.
Bos en Lommerweg 191, www.podiummozaiek.nl, tel. 020-5800380, open theater café Sun-Thur 9:30am-midnight, Fri-Sat 9:30am-1am, see website for performance timings, sandwich €5.75, Tram 19 Bos en Lommerweg

㉕ Mention the **Westerpark**, and Amsterdammers think first of the Westergasterrein, but the park is also worth a visit. It's spacious, with plenty of water, undulating lawns, and a children's zoo. The construction of the park began in 1890, a number of years after the earlier Willemspoort Station was closed and from where for 35 years trains departed for Haarlem on the first Dutch railway. After the former gasworks closed in 1967, the site was so polluted that the upper layer of soil had to be removed before it could be transformed into the park you'll find today, which is now ideal for a stroll or some grassy relaxation.
Westerpark, Tram 10 Van Limburg Stirumstraat

㉙ **Het Ketelhuis** (The Boiler House) is also known as "the canteen of Dutch film and TV," but the cinema also shows quality European films. If you're tired of no longer being able to find popcorn at many cinemas, here you can have dinner—the menu changes daily.
Pazzanistraat 4, www.ketelhuis.nl, tel. 020-6840090, see website for film showings, movie €10, Tram 5 Van Limburg Stirumstraat

㉛ This bathhouse was built in 1916 for workers from the Spaarndammerbuurt. Now the **Hammam,** with its several pools, is open to everyone.
Zaanstraat 88, www.hammamamsterdam.nl, tel. 020-6814818, open Mon 6-10pm (men), Tue-Fri noon-10pm (women), Sat-Sun noon-10pm (women), entrance €17, Tram 3 Haarlemmerplein

WALK **5**

OOST & DE PIJP

ABOUT THE WALK

On this walk, you'll encounter a cultural melting pot that's also rich in history, from typical Amsterdam markets to Jewish traditions. There are many trendy foreign restaurants that offer lunch or dinner. Artis, Amsterdam's zoo, is also on this walk—for children, combine a stop there with the fascinating and often-overlooked Tropenmuseum (Museum of the Tropics).

THE NEIGHBORHOODS

Oost (East) is perhaps Amsterdam's most varied neighborhood. Here you'll find the **Indische buurt,** where street names and the **Tropenmuseum** recall a colonial past. Hip and exotic blend perfectly here—on the Javastraat, there are a growing number of trendy coffeehouses, boutiques, and restaurants interspersed with multicultural shops. The locals actively encourage this melting pot and rightly so. What could be nicer than buying reasonably priced vegetables and then drinking a perfect cup of coffee nearby?

Next is the Dapperbuurt, with its genuine old Amsterdam character and the famous **Dappermarkt. Linnaeusstraat** has a nice bar on every corner. The **Dapperbuurt** borders on the green **Plantagebuurt,** where, in addition to **Artis** zoo, you'll find the former Jewish Quarter. Jewish traditions are respectfully preserved at the **Jewish Historical Museum** and the **synagogue.** At the **Verzetsmuseum** (Dutch Resistance Museum), you can learn all about Jewish history and World War II.

In the middle of all this lies the vibrant **Oosterpark,** where the cultures of East Amsterdam come together. The monuments in the park recall a turbulent history of slavery, as well as more recent events, such as the 2004 murder of Dutch film director Theo van Gogh. At the Tropenmuseum, which sits at the edge of the park, you can discover more about cultures and customs from around the world.

Oost can be combined with **De Pijp,** a melting pot of yuppies and market sellers. The De Pijp area has since become very trendy, as it was once a district for blue-collar workers. There's always something happening on the **Albert Cuypmarkt,** with its many shops, stalls, and cafés. In the middle of the market you'll find the **statue of André Hazes,** who was born and raised in the area. **Sarphatipark** is situated near the market and is one of the city's smaller but perhaps most beautiful parks.

SHORT ON TIME? HERE ARE THE HIGHLIGHTS:

13 BIERTUIN + 15 TROPENMUSEUM +
18 HORTUS BOTANICUS + 28 ALBERT CUYPMARKT
+ 35 SARPHATIPARK

TIPS

// A melting pot
of cultures
// Walk this route on a
market day
// The best walk for
children

OOST & DE PIJP

LEGEND

● >> SIGHTS & ATTRACTIONS

● >> FOOD & DRINK

● >> SHOPPING

● >> MORE TO EXPLORE

✦ >> WALK HIGHLIGHT

WALK 5 DESCRIPTION (approx. 7 mi/11 km with detour)

Start at Drover's Dog ❶. From here cross the square, turn left down Sumatrastraat, and turn right onto Javastraat ❷ ❸. On Javaplein check out a cozy bar/restaurant ❹ and behind it another interesting restaurant ❺ and a vintage shop ❻. Cross the street and turn down Borneostraat to Amsterdam East's hotspot ❼. Then cross the street diagonally and take the first left. Turn right onto Javastraat ❽ ❾. Walk under the railway to the Dappermarkt ❿. Follow the road ⓫ ⓬. Turn right on Linnaeusstraat ⓭ ⓮. Continue and cross the road at the roundabout for the Tropenmuseum ⓯. From here, decide whether to follow the optional detour or take the regular route.

Detour (approx. 2 mi/3 km): Turn onto Mauritskade, cross the first bridge and follow Plantage Middenlaan ⓰ ⓱ ⓲. Continue until you reach Meester Visserplein, bear left, then turn left after the synagogue ⓳ onto Jonas Daniël Meijerplein ⓴. Cross the bridge and turn left onto Hortusplantsoen. Bear right at the fork and cross over Plantage Muidergracht. Walk through the Plantagebuurt until you reach Plantage Middenlaan again. Head to the Tropenmuseum to continue the route.

Regular route: Follow Linnaeusstraat to the entrance of the Oosterpark ㉑. Walk through the park and exit at the monument to slavery. Walk to the intersection with Eerste Oosterparkstraat ㉒. Walk down Beukenweg to Beukenplein ㉓. Turn back and head left onto Tweede Oosterparkstraat. Take the first right and at the end of the street turn left onto Eerste Oosterparkstraat. Continue to Wibautstraat, cross the road, turn right and take the second left ㉔. Exit the street over Nieuwe Amstelbrug, continue on Ceintuurbaan ㉕ and take the second right to De Pijp. Continue until you reach Tweede Jan Steenstraat. Turn left and then right onto Eerste Sweelinckstraat ㉖. Turn right onto Govert Flinckstraat, then take the first left. Continue to the concept store ㉗, or turn earlier onto Albert Cuypstraat ㉘ ㉙ ㉚. Turn right onto Eerste van der Helststraat and walk to Gerard Doustraat ㉛ ㉜. Cross Ferdinand Bolstraat and continue on Saenredamstraat ㉝. Turn left onto Frans Halsstraat, then left again on Govert Flinckstraat. Take a right at Eerste van der Helststraat ㉞ and walk to Sarphatipark ㉟, entering through the first entrance on the right. Follow the path to reach the exit. Turn left and walk a short distance ㊱, then turn right onto Ceintuurbaan ㊲ ㊳. Turn left on Ferdinand Bolstraat and walk to Cornelis Troostplein ㊴.

SIGHTS & ATTRACTIONS

❸ Architect Hendrik Petrus Berlage didn't design only Amsterdam's stock exchange—he also built the **Berlageblokken** (1911-1914) to accommodate workers. The complex was inspired by British social housing and today these are historically listed buildings. It was important to include sufficient greenery, so the accommodation includes small parks as well as inner courtyards with gardens. The apartments underwent a substantial renovation at the end of the 1960s.
Balistraat, Benkoelenstraat, Javaplein, Javastraat En Langkatstraat, not open to the public, Tram 14 Javaplein

❶❺ The **Tropenmuseum** (Museum of the Tropics) is a unique museum housed in a beautiful building where you can wander through lifelike replicas of dwellings, rooms, and shops from countries around the world. It houses an enormous collection of objects from numerous cultures—a door from Marrakech, an altar from Mexico, African musical instruments. That's not all that this inspiring museum has to offer, though. There are films and wonderful interactive and temporary exhibitions with special activities for children.
Linnaeusstraat 2, www.tropenmuseum.nl, tel. 088-0042840, open Tue-Sun 10am-5pm, also open on Mon during school holidays , entrance €15, Tram 19 1e Van Swindenstraat

❶❼ The **Verzetsmuseum** Amsterdam (Resistance Museum) is located in the Plancius building, opposite the entrance to Artis zoo. In this permanent exhibition a lifelike decor of city streets and a floor-to-ceiling visual display help create an atmosphere reminiscent of Amsterdam during WWII. Authentic historical objects, photos, documents, film, and audio tell the story of the people who lived here during wartime. There's also an interactive children's museum where the story is told through the eyes of children.
Plantage Kerklaan 61, www.verzetsmuseum.org, tel. 020-6202535, open Sat-Sun 11am-5pm, Mon-Fri 10am-5pm, entrance €11, Tram 14 Artis

❶❾ This **Portuguese Synagogue** (also called Esnoga or Snoge) is situated in the heart of Amsterdam's former Jewish Quarter. The first Jews to settle in Amsterdam in the 16th century came from Spain and Portugal. The synagogue not only continues to fulfill its original function, but the interior has been preserved in its original state. In the 17th century, Snoge was the world's

largest synagogue and formed part of an extensive synagogue complex. Today, the other synagogues house the Jewish Historical Museum.

Mr. Visserplein 3, www.portugesesynagoge.nl, open Apr-Oct Sun-Thur 10am-5pm, Fri 10am-4pm, Nov-Mar Sun-Thur 10am-4pm, Fri 10am-2pm, entrance €12, Tram 14 Mr. Visserplein, Metro 51, 53, 54 Waterlooplein

20 At the **Joods Historisch Museum** (Jewish Historical Museum), you can learn about the culture, religion, and history of the Jewish people who lived in the Netherlands and its former colonies. The museum has a large collection of war documents. Many personal belongings such as letters, diaries, and photos are also on display, along with films.

Nieuwe Amstelstraat 1, www.jhm.nl, tel. 020-5310380, open daily 11am-5pm, entrance €15, includes all five locations of the Jewish Cultural Quarter, Tram 14 Mr. Visserplein, Metro 51, 53, 54 Waterlooplein

25 Take a good look at the **Huis met de Kabouters** (House with the Gnomes) because there's a lot more to it than meets the eye. The architect designed the three houses in 1884, giving free rein to his imagination. It has Swiss

chalet-style elements, with abundant wood carving, most striking of which are a pair of green gnomes playing with a ball. Almost as old as the house is the associated tale—that now and then the gnomes toss the ball—so that every so often you'll find the ball in the hands of the other gnome.
Ceintuurbaan 251-255, not open to the public, Tram 3 Van Woutstraat, Tram 4 Ceintuurbaan

❷❾ Probably the most famous inhabitant of de Pijp was born on the third floor of No. 67 Gerard Doustraat. The beloved Dutch folk singer **André Hazes** spent his youth in and around the Albert Cuypmarkt. It was here he drank his first beer, and it was here he was discovered in 1959. His **statue** was unveiled in September 2005, the day his ashes were fired into the air with 10 flares. Fans still place a beer or some flowers next to his statue.
Albert Cuypstraat, Tram 4 Stadhouderskade

FOOD & DRINK

❶ Start the day with a taste of Australia. **Drover's Dog** has a super-friendly Aussie atmosphere. And Australians know how to breakfast—choose from sweet, savory, spicy, or crispy. "Bog in" to the Drover's own full-cooked *brekkie*—a *ripper* combination of fried eggs, sausages, tomatoes, spinach, and mushrooms. "Don't knock it till you've tried it!" That goes for the *roo*, too!
Eerste Atjehstraat 62, www.drovers-dog.com, tel. 020-3703784, open Tue-Thur 11am-11:30pm, Fri-Sun 10am-11:30pm, brunch €10, main course €18, Tram 1, 3 Muiderpoortstation

❹ **Badhuis Javaplein** was one of the last bathhouses to be built in Amsterdam (1942) and is now a trendy restaurant-café. The building also previously housed a Hindu temple and a secondhand shop. Today it has again become the meeting place for the neighborhood. Shower heads have made space for beer taps and an open fireplace. Only the tiled wall behind the bar recalls the place where women once washed.
Javaplein 21, badhuis-javaplein.com, tel. 020-6651226, open Mon-Thur 10-1am, Fri-Sun 10-3am, €15, Tram 14 Javaplein

5 One of the best places to sample high-quality Dutch food in atmospheric surroundings is at **Wilde Zwijnen** (Wild Boar). Seasonal dishes are made, as far as practicable, with local Dutch produce. In autumn the menu includes dishes with such wonderful names as *in Limburgs grottenbierbeslag gefrituurde mergelgrotchampignons* (fried Limburg Mergel cave mushrooms in beer batter) or venison stew. Reserve a place and look for your name chalked on the table.
Javaplein 23, www.wildezwijnen.com, tel. 020-4633043, open Mon-Thur 6-10:15pm, Fri-Sun 12-4pm & 6-10:15pm, three course menu €30.50, Tram 14 Javaplein

12 Anyone who has visited Suriname (a former Dutch colony) knows that **Roopram Roti**'s *roti* ("pancake" with a spicy filling) is among the best. It was a smart move on the owner's part to export the concept. And with the Oosterpark just around the corner, you can have a Surinamese picnic in the park.
Eerste Van Swindenstraat 4, www.roopramroti.nl, tel. 020-6932902, open Tue-Sun 2pm-9pm, from €5, Tram 19 1e Van Swindenstraat

13 You'll have to try really hard to think of a beer that's not on this beer garden's menu. On offer at **De Biertuin** are beers such as Brouwerij 't IJ, wheat beer (witbier) and specials with names such as Snake Dog and Lamme Goedzak (Drunken Softy). In the evening, the restaurant serves six main courses, including spit-roasted chicken.
Linnaeusstraat 29, www.debiertuin.nl, tel. 020-6650956, open Sun-Thur 11am-1am, Fri-Sat 11am-3am, beer from €2.20, Tram 19 1e Van Swindenstraat

14 On the corner across from the Tropenmuseum you'll find **Louie Louie,** an all-day café with a fantastic outdoor seating area where you can easily spend hours. The menu features dishes inspired by South American cuisine, including tacos, quesadillas and of course, a variety of meat dishes. They make a mean cocktail, or you can order their 1.5-quart pitcher of sangria. Perfect if you want to raise a glass with friends.
Linnaeusstraat 11, louielouie.nl, tel. 020-3702981, open Sun-Thur 9am-1am, Fri-Sat 9am-3am, mains from €12, sangria pitcher €21.50, Tram 1, 3 Alexanderplein, Tram 19 1e Van Swindenstraat

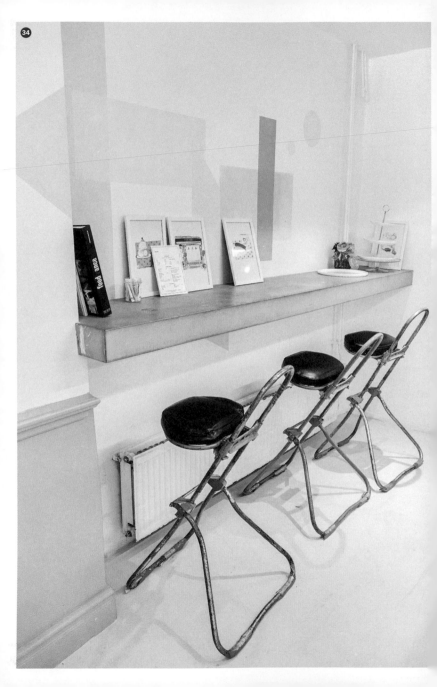

㉒ Bar Bukowski is a must for its roaring '20s interior and delicious breakfast. But these are not the only reasons it has become a social hotspot in East Amsterdam. Everything fits—from the rough-intellectual interior, inspired by writer and lover of alcohol Charles Bukowski, to Henry's cocktail bar and the fresh juices. As Bukowski himself wrote, "There's always a reason to drink!" Oosterpark 10, www.barbukowski.nl, tel. 020-3701685, open Mon-Thur 8am-1am, Fri 8am-3am, Sat 9am-3am, Sun 9am-1am, sandwich €6, Tram 1, 3 Beukenweg

㉓ To taste, to smell, and to see, is to know that the owners of **Coffee Bru** got their inspiration from South Africa's coffee bars. Plants grow between the characteristic furniture and the smell of coffee hangs in the air while homemade banana bread and cakes and pies—devil's food and key lime—line the counter. Visiting tea lovers drink Chinese leaf tea called Chief Monkey, a brand established by one of the owners. Beukenplein 14, www.coffeebru.nl, tel. 020-7519956, open Mon-Fri 8am-6pm, Sat-Sun 9am-6pm, coffee from €2.30, Tram 1, 3 Beukenweg

㉔ De Ruyschkamer is a Berlin-style café, with soft drinks and beers to match. Concoct your super healthy drink at the juice bar, lounge with your pizza on the couch, or sample macaroons with flavors beyond your wildest dreams, such as cinnamon with a ganache of cherries and soft caramel. Alternatively, you might like to try your hand at the legendary German bingo or contemplate buying one of the beautiful pieces of furniture. Or perhaps you'd rather just have a cup of coffee while perusing the newspaper at the reading table. Ruyschstraat 34, www.deruyschkamer.nl, tel. 020-6703622, open Wed & Thur 5pm-1am, Fri-Sat 5pm-2am, Sun 3pm-11pm, from €1.90, Tram 3 Wibautstraat

㉖ The trendy **Little Collins** is a tribute to its Melbourne namesake, which means an impressive brunch and dinner menu. You can brunch here all day long on cauliflower hashes, baked puddings, and Florentines. On Thursdays and Fridays, there is also dinner—choose from an international selection of small dishes. Bloody Marys make an excellent accompaniment to brunch, and for dinner choose from an extensive selection of wines. Eerste Sweelinckstraat 19, www.littlecollins.nl, tel. 020-6732293, open Mon-Tue 9am-4pm, Wed-Sun 9am-10pm, lunch €13, Tram 3 Van Woutstraat, Tram 4 Ceintuurbaan

30 "Come as you are, pay what you like," is the motto at **Café Trust,** a peaceful oasis in the heart of the busy Albert Cuypmarkt. You pay what you feel the food is worth.
Albert Cuypstraat 210, tel. 020-7371532, opening times vary, prices vary, Tram 4 Stadhouderskade

33 Casual yet luxurious with a menu full of great food and wines, **Maris Piper** feels very much like a Parisian bistro. However, it's in the middle of the Amsterdam neighborhood De Pijp. The menu has something for everyone and includes seafood platters, beef Wellington, and of course steak-frites. The kitchen, located in the back of the restaurant, features a "chef's table"—an exclusive table with a separate menu. Great for an exceptional dining experience!
Frans Halsstraat 76hs, maris-piper.com, tel. 020-7372479, open daily noon-10:30pm, chef's menu €115, Tram 24 Marie Heinekenplein, Metro 52 De Pijp

34 At **My Little Patisserie** you can choose from an assortment of mouthwatering pastries. Owner Audrey used to have a career in marketing, and when she needed a change of pace she enrolled at the prestigious Parisian bakers' school École de Boulangerie et de Patisserie. She eventually moved to Amsterdam for love, and her dream became a reality with the opening of her own French patisserie. Enjoy yours indoors in the petit café or outdoors in the Sarphatipark around the corner.
Eerste Van Der Helststraat 63, mylittlepatisserie.nl, tel. 020-4706949, open Mon-Fri 9:30am-5:30pm, Sat 9am-6pm, pastries from €4, Tram 3 2e Van Der Helststraat, Metro 52 De Pijp

36 Lots of wood, an open floor plan, the food and clothing, all conjure Scandinavia—clean and sustainable. Scandinavia has a vibrant, sophisticated coffee culture, which you can experience for yourself here at the **Scandinavian Embassy.** The coffee comes from small coffee producers in Stockholm, Helsingborg, and Oslo, among other places. On the menu are dishes such as spit-roasted lamb, fermented herring, and Danish cheese.
Sarphatipark 34, www.scandinavianembassy.nl, tel. 068-1600140, open Mon-Fri 8am-6pm, Sat-Sun 9am-6pm, from €13, Tram 3 2e Van Der Helststraat, Metro 52 De Pijp

37 SLA raises the average salad to delicious new heights. Some of the vegetables (as far as possible organic) are grown along the wall and in the business's own greenhouse. The accompanying meat, fish, grain, and dairy products are all organic. In the large industrial interior, healthy eating can be combined perfectly with a glass of wine or beer, though it's not easy to choose from the wide variety of salads on offer. SLA also has its own lab where you can take inspiring workshops.

Ceintuurbaan 149, www.ilovesla.com, tel. 020-7893080, open daily 11am-9pm, from €8, Tram 3 2e Van Der Helststraat, Metro 52 De Pijp

38 The former Ceintuurtheater dates back to the 1920s and was closed for a long time, but after a thorough renovation it now houses **CT Coffee & Coconuts.** Grab a bite at this city venue with three floors where trendy Amsterdam hangs out with good coffee and healthy food.

Ceintuurbaan 282, www.ctamsterdam.nl, tel. 020-3541104, open daily 8:30am-11pm, full breakfast €10.50, Tram 3, 12, 24 De Pijp, Metro 52 De Pijp

ALL
THE
LUCK
IN
THE
WORLD
.NL

friendly roots of the Scandinavian cuisine. We are also pairing coffee and enhancing the overall culinary experience

Dominika explores the relationship between symmetry and asymmetry, focusing on form. She develops fashion collections from different techniques.

We also offer courses — be it modern desserts, fish or knife-technique, coffee brewing and co

Welcome!
Scandi
Scandi

SHOPPING

❷ **Java Bookshop** was once a bit out of place in this neighborhood, but the hidden gem of a bookshop has now come into its own. Take time to browse among a wide selection of Dutch and English literature, cookbooks, and children's books, all in a homey atmosphere. The enthusiastic staff is happy to let you make up your mind over a cup of coffee and something tasty.
Javastraat 145, www.javabookshop.nl, tel. 020-4634993, open Tue-Fri 10am-6pm, Sat 10am-5pm, Tram 14 Javaplein

❻ Step into this shop that's hidden behind the baths, and you'll find you've stepped back into rooms from the 1950s and '60s. Everything at **Jansen Vintage** is for sale. All items have been carefully curated, from the lamps to the glassware, the tableware and the special bedside tables, and the rough stools and furniture from known and unknown brands.
Javaplein 31, www.jansenvintage.nl, tel. 061-0125018, open Wed-Sat 11am-6pm, Tram 14 Javaplein

❽ **Hartje Oost** (Heart of East) is one of the latest additions to the Javastraat. It's a coffee boutique, which means good coffee, fashionable clothing, fresh sandwiches and cakes, and handmade jewelry. The boutique's owners aim to sell only products that tell a story—ecological, sustainable, fair trade, local, and original. They combine foods from businesses in and around Javastraat, such as Peking Duck from the Asian shop, with sourdough bread from De bakker van Oost.
Javastraat 23, www.hartjeoost.nl, tel. 020-2332137, open Mon-Fri 9am-6:30pm, Sat-Sun 9am-6pm, Tram 14 Javaplein

❾ Tough guys can confidently stroll into **Div. Herenkabinet.** The selection is uncluttered and clean and is only from the most stylish, trendiest brands (including Pointer, Obey, and Carhartt). The owner can tell you something about everything, from the Japanese jeans to the Swiss knives, and from the Swedish backpacks to the Belgian sunglasses.
Javastraat 8, www.divamsterdam.com, tel. 020-6944084, open Mon-Fri 10am-6:30pm, Sat 10am-6pm, Sun 12-6pm, Tram 1, 3 Dapperstraat, Tram 14 Zeeburgerdijk

⓫ Now that secondhand has become "vintage," recycled clothing has largely become unaffordable. But things are done differently at **We Are Vintage** (note the ceiling!)—clothing can be purchased by the pound, and it's still good quality. Much of the collection is sorted by color and type. Lovers of suede and leather will feel right at home.

Eerste Van Swindenstraat 43, www.wearevintage.nl, tel. 020-7852777, open Mon-Wed & Fri-Sat 11am-7pm, Thu 11am-8pm, Sun noon-6pm, Tram 19 1e Van Swindenstraat

㉗ Hutspot (Stew) stocks only products by new, exciting brands, designers, artists, and entrepreneurs, including clothing, accessories, furniture, and household items. There is also an industrial-style bar on the second floor, where you can hang out with special beers and exclusive cocktails until the early hours of the weekend. Hotspot has a second branch on Rozengracht.

Van Woustraat 4, www.hutspot.com, tel. 020-2231331, open Mon-Sat 10am-7pm, Sun noon-6pm, Tram 4 Stadhouderskade

㉛ Fans of fashion from the 1940s through '60s can't help but pay a visit to **The Girl can't help it.** This pink boutique is filled to the brim with brand new retro designs that would've suited iconic figures such as Marilyn Monroe and Audrey Hepburn. It's all feminine, elegant, and sexy. The staff here loves to help find an outfit that will enhance your figure and leave you feeling fabulous. The owner has her own line of skirts and can customize clothing in her atelier for the perfect fit.

Gerard Doustraat 87, www.thegirlcanthelpit.nl, tel. 020-2333399, open Tue-Sat 11am-6pm, Tram 24 Marie Heinekenplein

㉜ All the Luck in the World is the perfect place to find unique gifts for someone—or for you. From beautiful new and vintage home accessories to postcards, posters, kitchen gadgets, and bags. The shop sells Danish design and unique pieces made by Dutch designers. Everything is displayed and combined beautifully, making you spoilt for choice. Their own jewelry line features delicate necklaces, bracelets, earrings, and rings made of silver, or gold plate.

Gerard Doustraat 86hs, www.alltheluckintheworld.nl, tel. 065-5022230, open Sun 1pm-6pm, Mon noon-6pm, Tue-Wed & Fri-Sat 11am-6pm, Thu 11am-8pm, Tram 24 Marie Heinekenplein, Metro 52 De Pijp

MORE TO EXPLORE

7 **Studio/K** is a space for film, theater, music, food, and drink—all brought together in an old trade school, with a colorful clientele. For a perfect night out, purchase the "film package," which consists of dinner (one main), and a movie ticket.

Timorplein 62, www.studio-k.nu, tel. 020-6920422, open Sun-Thur 11am-1am, Fri & Sat 11am-3am, movie €9.50, dinner & movie €17, Tram 14 Javaplein

10 The **Dappermarkt** has been named the best market in the Netherlands several times. You'll find endless stalls that sell wares from around the world. What you won't find are many tourists, as this market has a distinct neighborhood feel to it.

Dappermarkt, www.dappermarkt.nl, open Mon-Sat 10am-5pm, Tram 1, 3 Dapperstraat

16 With or without the kids, **Artis** is fun. The zoo first opened in 1838 to bring nature closer to the city, and it's still popular today. Right next door you'll find

café-restaurant Plantage. Its stunning 19th century conservatory looks out upon the freely accessible Artisplein (Artis Square).

Plantage Kerklaan 38-40, www.artis.nl, tel. 020-5233670, open daily Nov-Feb 9am-5pm, Mar-Oct 9am-6pm, Jun-Aug every Sat 9am until sunset, entrance €23, Tram 14 Artis

18 Dating from 1638, the **Hortus Botanicus** is one of the oldest botanical gardens in the world. It includes an exotic mixture of 6,000 plants spread over an enormous outdoor garden and several greenhouses.

Plantage Middenlaan 2a, www.dehortus.nl, tel. 020-6259021, open daily 10am-5pm, entrance €8.50, Tram 14 Artis

21 In the **Oosterpark** you'll find the national monument that recalls the history of slavery and *De Schreeuw* (*The Scream*) sculpture that was created in memory of film director Theo van Gogh, who was murdered nearby in 2004 by a Muslim extremist. There are also a number of festivals held here during summertime.

Oosterpark, Tram 1, 3 Linnaeusstraat, Tram 19 Wijttenbachstraat

28 Stroll down the **Albert Cuypmarkt,** which is alive with the cries of market stall holders. There is an array of snacks—everything from waffles, pancakes, to fresh stroopwafel. Also explore behind the stalls, where there are some interesting shops.

Albert Cuypstraat, www.albertcuypmarkt.nl, open Mon-Sat 9am-5pm, Tram 4 Stad-houderskade, Metro 52 De Pijp

35 In the mid-19th century, the original plan was to build Centraal Station at this location. Fortunately, Samuel Sarphati, a Jewish doctor and philanthropist who initiated many projects to improve the quality of life in Amsterdam, came up with a better idea to create this English landscape park, the **Sarphatipark.**

Sarphatipark, Tram 3 2e Van Der Helststraat, Metro 52 De Pijp

39 Beer doesn't come fresher than at **Brouwerij Troost**. It is brewed on-site by enthusiastic young beer lovers. They picked the perfect location—a former monastery with a beautiful courtyard. The beers go down easy, combining perfectly with meaty menu items such as burgers, steaks, and spare ribs.

Cornelis Troostplein 23, www.brouwerijtroost.nl, tel. 020-7371028, open Mon-Thur 4pm-1am, Fri 4pm-3am, Sat 2pm-3am, Sun 2pm-midnight, beer from €2.50, Tram 12 Cornelis Troostplein

EILANDEN & NOORD

ABOUT THE WALK

This walk takes you through what was once a lively port. On the eastern islands (Eilanden) you'll pass architectural highlights and interesting bridges. Once you've crossed the IJ (the river dividing the center of Amsterdam from Amsterdam Noord), you'll discover Amsterdam's trendiest neighborhood, with its raw industrial edge and countless culinary and art initiatives. Cycling this route is also ideal—you can take in a larger area of Noord.

THE NEIGHBORHOODS

"If you come from north of the IJ, you're not one of us," was long the view of many Amsterdammers. But times have changed. Today, the ferries are busy transporting trendy passengers to and from the north. It's the place to be for the **IJ-hallen,** which houses Europe's largest indoor flea market, the futuristic **EYE** film museum, and industrial cafés, restaurants, and vintage shops. **Noord** is Amsterdam's Brooklyn and is increasingly listed as one of the world's trendiest neighborhoods.

It still has space for creativity and relaxation. There's the recently constructed promenade along the IJ and the **Oeverpark,** from where you can view the city and clear your head. Cafés and restaurants are spacious, with entire gardens and urban beaches where you won't be bothered by screeching trams or hordes of visitors.

What was once a no-go area is now attracting more and more young families to the other side of the IJ. You're outside the city but can still reach it in no time. And today, there's always something going on. Creative entrepreneurs and businesses are springing up everywhere, attracted by the charm of Noord with its raw edge and great old shipyards with an industrial vibe.

Java-eiland and **KNSM-eiland,** prized as new architectural highlights, have also become popular, conjuring up today's Rotterdam with their trading and shipping history. Here you can chill out on the quays and check out the architecture. More and more, well-educated Amsterdammers are moving here with their kids.

SHORT ON TIME? HERE ARE THE HIGHLIGHTS:
⑦ SCHEEPVAARTMUSEUM + ⑮ ROEST + ⑰ JAVA-EILAND + ㉚ EYE + ㊱ NOORDERLICHT CAFÉ

TIPS
// Route through Amsterdam's trendiest neighborhood
// For architecture lovers
// Good biking route

EILANDEN & NOORD

1. SkyLounge Amsterdam
2. Centrale Bibliotheek
3. Hannekes Boom
4. Scheepskameel
5. NEMO
6. Museumhaven
7. **Het Scheepvaartmuseum**
8. De Gooyer
9. Brouwerij 't IJ
10. de werkwinkel +meer
11. CP113
12. Coffee and Friends
13. Olie & Zo
14. Rosa & Rita
15. **Roest**
16. Lloyd Hotel
17. **Java-eiland**
18. De Negen Bruggen
19. KNSM-eiland
20. Kanis & Meiland 3.0
21. Kompaszaal
22. Hangar
23. Hotel de Goudfazant
24. FC Hyena
25. Stork
26. Il Pecorino
27. Café Modern
28. Tolhuistuin
29. The Coffee Virus
30. **EYE**
31. Oeverpark
32. Blom & Blom
33. Neef Louis
34. Van Dijk en Ko
35. IJ-hallen
36. **Noorderlicht Café**
37. Pllek
38. Woodies at Berlin
39. IJ-kantine

LEGEND

- \>> SIGHTS & ATTRACTIONS
- \>> FOOD & DRINK
- \>> SHOPPING
- \>> MORE TO EXPLORE
- \>> WALK HIGHLIGHT

0   300 yds
0   300 m

WALK 6

© MOON.CO

WALK 6 DESCRIPTION (approx. 11 mi/18 km)

Start at Oosterdokskade ❶. From the library ❷, turn left and, at the
intersection, walk to Hannekes Boom ❸ or continue to Scheepskameel ❹.
Follow the route to the right for NEMO ❺. Walk around the museum and
turn right at Oosterdok ❻. Follow the water to the Scheepvaartmuseum ❼.
Continue to Kattenburgergracht and follow this street until you reach the flour
mill ❽ and the brewery ❾. Walk back to the bridge, cross the canal and walk
down Czaar Peterstraat ❿ ⓫ ⓬ ⓭. At the end of the street, before the
railway, turn left to the former Werkspoor factory grounds, then go left again ⓮.
Turn right, walk around the building to Roest ⓯ and continue to the overpass.
Turn right under the railway until you reach Piet Heinkade. Cross the road and
after the tram stop, turn left to cross the tram tracks. Now you're in
Rietlandpark. Continue to Lloydplein via Lloyd Hotel ⓰ to Veemkade and turn
right. Follow the road and turn left over the bridge to Java-eiland ⓱. Turn left
and walk through Bogortuin to the Nine Bridges ⓲. Walk back through the
gardens and continue to Levantkade on the KNSM-eiland ⓳ ⓴. Turn left onto
Levantplein, then right and left again onto KNSM-laan ㉑. Walk to Azartplein and
take the free ferry from here to Amsterdam Noord. Once there, you can sit on
the waterfront ㉒ ㉓ ㉔. Follow the water, turn left onto Aambeeldstraat and at
the intersection, turn left onto Gedempte Hamerkanaal. On the industrial site
you'll find a fish restaurant ㉕. Walk back, turn left onto Gedempte Hamerkanaal
until you reach the water, then turn right. Take the first left past the
supermarket, then turn left. Take Motorwal to Noordwal, walking along the
water to where the ferry docks. Turn right and take the first left to Sixhavenweg.
Follow until you reach the water. Cross the sluices, turn left and walk along the
water to Buiksloterweg. Take a right for some good restaurants ㉖ ㉗. Turn back
and walk along the canal to Tolhuistuin ㉘. Follow the route in front of the
building, cross the bridge and turn right for coffee ㉙. Walk toward IJ and turn
right via IJ-promenade toward EYE ㉚. Walk along the waterfront and into the
Oeverpark ㉛. Turn onto Bundlaan and bear right on Grasweg. Turn left onto
Asterweg and then right on Chrysantenstraat ㉜. Continue until the end of
the road, turning left onto Distelweg, and continue until you can turn right over
the canal. After the bridge, take the first left ㉝ ㉞. Continue and finish on the
NDSM-wharf ㉟ ㊱ ㊲ ㊳ ㊴.

SIGHTS & ATTRACTIONS

6 The **Museumhaven** gives you a good idea of what Amsterdam looked like during the 17th century—ships from the navy moored here, and it was also home to the Dutch East India Company's shipyard. The port was an important hub for inland navigation until well into the 20th century. Today it's the final resting place of ships aged 50-150 years old, including barges, clippers, luxurious motor boats, and tugs.

Oosterdok, between Nemo and Het Scheepvaartmuseum, www.museumhaven amsterdam.nl, always open, free, Tram 26 Muziekgebouw Bimhuis

7 There couldn't be a better location for **Het Scheepvaartmuseum** (The National Maritime Museum). From 1656 the building was used as a warehouse for Amsterdam's naval war fleet. Now you can view a selection of paintings, different types of ships, weapons, and old maps of the world. Outside you can climb on board a replica of a 1749 ship from the Dutch East India Company.

Kattenburgerplein 1, www.hetscheepvaartmuseum.nl, tel. 20-5232222, open daily 9am-5pm, entrance €15, Tram 26 Kattenburgerstraat, Bus 22, 246 Kadijksplein

8 Between the 17th and 19th centuries, the defensive walls of the Outer Singel canal were lined with windmills. The last mills were demolished around 1900, but Korenmolen **De Gooyer** managed to survive. Built in 1725, the mill played an important role until the end, grinding corn for the citizens of Amsterdam during World War II. Unfortunately, the mill is not open to visitors, but it's still a pretty sight in the middle of the city.

Funenkade 5, Tram 7 Hoogte Kadijk, Tram 14 Pontanusstraat

16 Drop into the Lloyd Hotel. This former jail is one of Europe's most unique hotels. The corridors of this building, listed on the historic register, are a delight to any design enthusiast. The hotel is also a cultural embassy—guests can gain a deeper insight into Dutch culture through art, workshops, lectures, and concerts.

Oostelijke Handelskade 34, www.lloydhotel.com, tel. 20-5613636, open daily, Tram 10, 26 Rietlandpark

Does the atmosphere on **Java-eiland** remind you of something? Yes, it's the center of Amsterdam with a modern twist. In the early 20th century, the Netherlands' Steamship Company, whose liners serviced the Dutch East Indies, was located on the artificial island in the IJ (the lake that is Amsterdam's waterfront). With decolonization, trade virtually stopped and the island fell into disuse. For a long time, it was occupied by squatters until everything was demolished in the 1990s. Now the island is covered with postmodern canal houses. Regular concerts and events take place at the head of the island.

Java-Eiland, Tram 7 Azartplein

18 The **Negen Bruggen** (Nine Bridges) over Java-eiland's four canals were designed with the aim of seamlessly fusing art, architecture, and construction. Belgian artists' duo Guy Rombouts and Monica Droste based the bridges on their own "Azart" alphabet. In this typeset, every letter is represented by a shaped line and a color. For example, "C" is for curve and citrus yellow. Together the lines form a word. Although the original intention was for the letters to be given different colors, the architects decided the result would be too toylike.
Java-Eiland, Tram 7 Azartplein

19 As with Java-eiland, **KNSM-eiland** was also an important location for trade and transport to the Dutch East Indies until the 1950s. The Royal Dutch Steamship Company (KNSM) was located here from 1903. Today, next to the modern, high-rise buildings you'll still find the doctor's house, the customs building, and the canteen of the Dutch Dock and Shipbuilding Company. The old statues and fountain of Amphitrite have also stood the test of time.
KNSM-Eiland, Tram 7 Azartplein

21 Around 1950, when competition from the airlines began in earnest, the Royal Dutch Steamship Company pulled out all the stops to win over travelers. The result was the **Kompaszaal** (Compass Hall), a luxurious arrivals and departure hall that breathes the grandeur of the ships from olden days, and where nowadays you can enjoy high tea or lunch. High tea is served Wednesdays through Sundays, with reservations only.
KNSM-Laan 311, www.kompaszaal.nl, tel. 020-4199596, open Sat & Sun 11am-1am, Wed 10am-5pm, Thur & Fri 10am-1am, high tea from €17.50, Tram 7 Azartplein

30 Watch a film or visit an exhibition at **EYE,** which now houses the Netherlands' largest film library with at least 46,000 films, 50,000 photos, and 41,500 posters. The futuristic building opened in 2012.
IJ Promenade 1, www.eyefilm.nl, tel. 020-5891400, open Sun-Thur 10am-10pm, Fri-Sat 10am-10pm, free entrance, film €10, Ferry 901, 907 Buiksloterweg, Ferry 902 Ijplein

31 Thanks to the **Oeverpark,** Amsterdam now finally has a promenade on the waterfront. The park includes an elm arboretum with 30 varieties of elm. There's a view across the IJ to the imposing Centraal Station, where the roof of the bus station has at least 4,500 sheets of glass.
Oeverpark, Ferry 901, 907 Buiksloterweg

FOOD & DRINK

❶ This is a piece of Manhattan on the Amsterdam waterfront. Enjoy a spectacular panoramic view of the city, the IJ, and North Amsterdam with coffee or cocktails in the **SkyLounge Amsterdam.**

Oosterdoksstraat 4, doubletree3.hilton.com, open Sun-Tue 11am-1am, Wed-Thur 11am-2am, Fri-Sat 11am-3am, sandwiches from €15, Tram 2, 4, 11, 12, 13, 14, 17, 24, 26 Centraal Station, Metro 51, 52, 53, 54 Centraal Station

❸ Amsterdam's trendiest know the way to this café-restaurant. **Hannekes Boom** has its own dock complete with a picnic terrace on the water. The food is organic, and on the weekend it's time to dance!

Dijksgracht 4, www.hannekesboom.nl, tel. 020-4199820, open Sun-Thur 10am-1am, Fri-Sat 10am-3am, from €16.50, Tram, 26 Muziekgebouw Bimhuis

❹ The folks at **Scheepskameel** pay close attention to high-quality food and to their patrons. The stark cuisine excels in pure, fresh, and familiar flavors. An extensive wine list features only German wine. The restaurant is a bright and open space in a beautiful building located in the naval yards (Marineterrein). The owners are known for their other restaurant Rijssel (Marcusstraat 52)— a popular fixture in the Amsterdam food scene.

Kattenburgerstraat 7, scheepskameel.nl, tel. 020-3379680, open Tue-Sat 6pm-1am, from €45, Tram 26 Muziekgebouw Bimhuis

❾ **Brouwerij 't IJ,** next to Korenmolen De Gooyer, brews the best beer in Amsterdam. Beer lovers come for beers with humorous names like *Natte* (wet) and *Zatte* (drunk), or seasonal beers called *Paas IJ* (Easter egg). On the weekend you can take a guided tour.

Funenkade 7, www.brouwerijhetij.nl, tel. 020-5286237, open daily 2pm-8pm, Fri-Sun guided tours in English 3:30pm, Dutch 4pm, beer €3, guided tour + 1 beer €4.50, Tram 7 Hoogte Kadijk, Tram 14 Pontanusstraat

⓬ **Coffee and Friends** is the perfect place to start your day with a great cup of coffee. The people who run this place are super friendly and will make you feel right at home. This cozy café has a laid-back vibe and great outdoor seating

area, where you can watch people, bicycles, and trams rush by. Their smoothie bowls are highly recommended!

Czaar Peterstraat 135, www.coffeeandfriends.nl, tel. 062-7262621, open Sat & Sun 9:30am-5pm, Mon 11am-5pm, Tue-Fri 8:30am-5pm, lunch €8.95, Tram 7 1e Leeghwaterstraat

⑭ Rosa & Rita likes to keep it simple. Choose from a pizza or steak—both are prepared on-site. Eat while sitting comfortably in the former warehouse, next to a wood fire. Fun fact: contrary to what you might think, Rosa and Rita are not the owners of this small establishment. It was named after two tankers built in 1935 when the area was still a shipyard.

Conradstraat 471, www.rosaenrita.nl, tel. 061-1122373, open Wed-Sun from 3pm, pizza €9.50, steak €12.50, Tram 7, 26 Rietlandpark, Tram 7 1e Leeghwaterstraat

⑳ Kanis & Meiland 3.0 could be described as the islanders' local pub. Non-islanders are also welcome for a beer or a board game.

Levantkade 127, www.kanisenmeiland.nl, tel. 020-7370674, open Mon-Fri 8:30am-1am, Sat-Sun 10am-1am, drinks from €2.20, Tram 7 Azartplein

㉒ If you arrive on the ferry from Azartplein, you'll see the beautiful hangar made of green and gray corrugated sheet metal come closer and closer. The letters *P-e-r-o-n-i* glisten from the rooftop, as **Hangar**'s sunny terrace beckons you to spend long summer nights on the waterfront. Industrial and tropical go hand in hand at this place that was once part of a booming harbor. Now you can come here to enjoy Mediterranean dishes from Southern Europe and North Africa. The flavors are pure and pleasantly surprising, and the menu changes with the seasons.

Aambeeldstraat 36, hangar.amsterdam, tel. 020-3638657, open Sun-Thur 10am-1am, Fri-Sat 10am-3am, three-course menu €34.50, Ferry 915 Zamenhofstraat, Bus 38 Hamerstraat

㉓ This gigantic hangar houses one of the best restaurants in Amsterdam. At **Hotel de Goudfazant** you can order a seasonal meal for a great price in a fine, relaxed atmosphere indoors. In the summer you can dine at the picnic tables that beckon from the waterside.

Aambeeldstraat 10, www.hoteldegoudfazant.nl, tel. 020-6365170, open Tue-Sun 6-10pm, three course menu €30, Ferry 915 Zamenhofstraat, Bus 38 Hamerstraat

㉕ **Stork** is a seafood restaurant with high ideals. Working with Stichting Vis&Seizoen (Fish and Season Institute), Stork ensures that the fish appearing on the menu are fresh caught daily. Consideration is also given to the way in which the fish are farmed or caught. Add to this the restaurant's industrial character, the view of the IJ, and the huge terrace, and you'll understand why this is the perfect place to enjoy a fish soup or sea bass.

Gedempt Hamerkanaal 201, www.restaurantstork.nl, tel. 020-6344000, open daily 11am-10:30pm, from €20, Ferry 902 Ijplein, Ferry 915 Zamenhofstraat, Metro 52 Noorderpark

㉖ You can't miss this bright-orange building on the water—though 10 years ago, a river cruiser somehow did miss it and sailed up onto the patio! At **Il Pecorino,** you can have a panini during the day, and a crispy, traditional Neapolitan pizza straight from the oven at night. In the summer it's lovely to sit on the sunny deck and look out over the IJ.

Noordwal 1, www.ilpecorino.nl, tel. 020-7371511, open daily 5pm-11pm, pizza €12, Ferry 901, 907 Buiksloterweg, Metro 52 Noorderpark

㉗ This place is a must-visit for foodies. But beware, at **Café Modern** you don't get to choose anything yourself. Instead, the chef will present you with four courses that are guaranteed to tickle your taste buds. The menu changes each day, and the dishes are always flavorful and highly original. Be sure to mention any dietary restrictions—they will be happy to adjust things to your taste. This beautifully decorated space used to be a bank. Be sure to visit the restrooms, as they are located inside the old vault.

Meidoornweg 2, https://modernamsterdam.nl, tel. 020-4940684, open Mon-Thur noon-midnight, Fri & Sat noon-1am, four course menu €40, Ferry 901, 907 Buiksloterweg, Ferry 902 Ijplein, Metro 52 Noorderpark

㉙ As the name suggests, **The Coffee Virus** is all about the coffee. Here, beans are roasted locally, and the selection changes on a regular basis. The quality, however, is consistently high: they aim for the perfect brew, served up exactly as you like it. Pies and lunch dishes are equally recommendable. The café is located inside A.Lab, a creative space where a lot of freelancers work.

Overhoeksplein 2, thecoffeevirus.nl, tel. 020-2442341, open Mon-Fri 9am-4:30pm, filtered coffee €4.50, Ferry 901, 907 Buiksloterweg

㉚ From the outside, **Noorderlicht Café** (Northern Lights Café) resembles a greenhouse, thanks to its glass dome. Inside you'll discover it's beautifully decorated with materials from town and country alike. The interesting location, live music, and menu all ensure that Noorderlicht is one of the finest places in Amsterdam. It's located at the NDSM shipyard, where ships were once built and repaired. The transformation of the shipyard is currently in full swing, with trendy cafés springing up everywhere.

NDSM Plein 102, www.noorderlichtcafe.nl, tel. 020-4922770, open daily from 11am, kitchen closes at 10pm, from €9.50, Ferry 903, 905, 906 NDSM, Bus 35, 36 Atatürk

㉛ Pllek is more than just a café and restaurant. The venue is marketed as a "creative hangout," where you can take yoga classes on weekends, watch films with a social conscience, or down a detox cocktail. It also serves sandwiches or meals made with local, organic, and sustainable produce. Outside the building, which has been largely constructed from shipping containers, you can relax on the beachlike terrace.

TT Neveritaweg 59, www.pllek.nl, open daily from 9:30am (kitchen closes at 10pm), from €17.50, Ferry 903, 905, 906 NDSM, Bus 35, 36 Atatürk

39 Built by NDSM's shipbuilders, the industrial **IJ-kantine** once formed the shipyard's office building, assembly yard, and canteen. When the canteen went bankrupt in the 1980s, the Unemployed Shipbuilders Association took over the building for use as a community center, where members could play cards and billiards and have a drink. Now you can have something to eat or drink in the colorfully decorated café-restaurant overlooking the IJ.

Mt. Odinaweg 15-17, www.ijkantine.nl, tel. 020-6337162, open daily from 9am, half a lobster €23.50, Ferry 903, 905, 906 NDSM, Bus 35, 36 Atatürk

SHOPPING

10 At **de werkwinkel +meer** (literally: the workshop and more) you can purchase unique designer items and artworks from artists all over the world. Lian Aelmans, founder of the shop, selects everything with care and consideration—and it shows with wares such as beautiful ceramics, stunning graphic prints, and fine jewelry. This is the perfect place to hunt for that all-important one-of-a-kind gift. Combine your visit with a walk around the Oostelijke Eilanden!

Czaar Peterstraat 104, www.dewerk-winkel.nl, tel. 020-3636972, open Tue-Fri 10am-6pm, Sat 11am-6pm, Tram 7 1e Leeghwaterstraat

① Czaar Peterstraat now has its own concept store in the form of **CP113.** Try a coffee from the roasting plant in Amsterdam-Noord, accompanied by a cake from the mobile Van Moss bakery, while taking a look at the clothing in this well laid-out shop. Hanging from the rails are a mix of vintage and new clothing originating from anywhere from Amsterdam to Scandinavia. The furniture is also for sale.

Czaar Peterstraat 113, cp-stores.com, tel. 020-2231976, open Tue-Sat 11am-6pm, Tram 7 Eerste Leeghwaterstraat

⑬ Debby's desire on setting up shop in this former launderette was to fill it with products that she herself would be delighted with. The result is **Olie & Zo** (Oils & So On), a specialty store selling high-quality products for the kitchen. There are at least eight kinds of oil in barrels, half of which are organic. The "& Zo" part of the shop is also worth a visit—its shelves display fresh bread, sausages, special cheeses, unusual mustards, and Himalayan salt.

Czaar Peterstraat 128, www.olieenzo.com, tel. 020-6223832, open Tue-Fri 10am-6pm, Sat 10am-5pm, Tram 7 Eerste Leeghwaterstraat

㉜ Brothers **Blom & Blom** share a passion for forgotten items: objects that had an industrial life but are destined to be scrapped. The brothers love to explore the former East Germany, scouring factories for forgotten gems. The furniture and lamps are given a second life in their workshops in Berlin or Amsterdam and are sold through the webshop and at this store. Every object comes with a document certifying the product's origin.

Chrysantenstraat 20a, www.blomandblom.com, tel. 020-7372691, open Wed-Fri 10am-5pm, every 1st and 3rd Sat of the month 11am-5pm, Ferry 900 Distelweg, Ferry 901, 907 Buiksloterweg, Ferry 902 Ijplein

㉝ You've never seen so many vintage, design, and industrial products as are in this warehouse. **Neef Louis** (Cousin Louis) is an expert in collecting fine furniture, lamps, and accessories: he's regularly invited to decorate shops, film

sets, and fairs (such as the famous Bread & Butter in Berlin). Louis's mission is to enable his customers to make something beautiful of their surroundings.
Papaverweg 46, www.neeflouis.nl, tel. 020-4869354, open Thur-Fri 10am-6pm, Sat 10am-5:30pm, Ferry 900 Distelweg, Bus 35, 36, 293 Floraweg, Bus 38 Klaprozenweg

34 The people behind **Van Dijk and Ko** like to visit Hungary and Romania because that's where they know they can find beautiful cabinets, chests of drawers, beds, and dressers that deserve a second life. Besides these showpieces, you'll also find imaginative, handmade lampshades and lamp stands from the Gezusters Stoop Lampenkappenatelier (Stoop Sisters Lampshade Studio) and a great book department. Everything here is unique, and the collection changes daily, so if something tickles your fancy, don't think about it too long!
Papaverweg 46, www.vandijkenko.nl, tel. 020-6841524, open Tue-Sat 10am-6pm, Sun noon-6pm, Ferry 900 Distelweg, Bus 35, 36, 293 Floraweg, Bus 38 Klaprozenweg

38 At this first furniture store in the NDSM shipyard, you'll find some vintage furniture plus numerous designs by Esther from **Woodies at Berlin.** Esther works with wood and steel and has three furniture lines—sleek, organic, and natural. The store displays her earlier work, or you can also get started on your own design with Esther's assistance. In addition to furniture and lighting, the store also sells fair-trade clothing.
Ms. Van Riemsdijkweg 51, www.woodiesatberlin.nl, tel. 064-3008100, open Sat noon-5pm, Ferry 903, 905, 906 NDSM, Bus 35, 36 Atatürk

MORE TO EXPLORE

2 The **Centrale** Openbare **Bibliotheek** Amsterdam (the Amsterdam public library) opened on the seventh day of the seventh month in 2007. It's the Netherlands' largest library. Although as a visitor it doesn't make sense to join the library, do drop in anyway. Admire the modern design, and above all check out the wonderful panoramic view of the city from the restaurant on the seventh floor.
Oosterdoksekade 143, www.oba.nl, tel. 020-5230900, open daily 10am-10pm, free, Tram 2, 4, 11, 12, 13, 14, 17, 24, 26 Centraal Station, Metro 51, 52, 53, 54 Centraal Station

5 **NEMO** is the largest science museum in the Netherlands. All manner of interactive scientific and technological installations are spread over five floors. Whizzkids, nerds, and adults alike—even those with little knowledge of science and technology—can happily spend a very entertaining afternoon here and learn something in the process. The roof terrace is open to all and is a great place for a drink.

Oosterdok 2, www.e-nemo.nl, tel. 020-5313233, open daily 10am-5:30pm, also on Mon during school holidays, roof terrace open until 7pm during summer, entrance €15, Tram 26 Muziekgebouw Bimhuis

15 **Roest** (Rust) opened a few years ago on the site where Dutch East India Company ships were once built. Today it's a combined café, theater, music venue, exhibition space, beach, and club. Buy snacks and drinks in a "camping shop" or double-decker bus, and head for the beach or restaurant.

Jacob Bontiusplaats, www.amsterdamroest.nl, open Sun-Thur 1am1-1am, Fri 4pm-3am, Sat 11am-3am, free, Tram 7, 26 Rietlandpark

24 Not a soccer team or football club, but a boutique cinema, complete with a petit-restaurant and wine bar—that's **FC Hyena.** You can watch the movie in one of two screening rooms while seated on homemade couches, and afterward it's discussion time. All this while enjoying some natural wine and tasty snacks from a wood-fired brick oven. You're even allowed to take food and drinks with you into the cinema. FC stands for "Film Club," but the interior is more reminiscent of a sports canteen, albeit it a very cool one!
Aambeeldstraat 24, fchyena.nl, tel. 020-3638502, open Sat-Sun noon-1am, Mon-Fri 4pm-1am, mains from €14, Ferry 915 Zamenhofstraat, Bus 38 Hamerstraat

28 For seventy years, this was the canteen for Shell employees. Today, the company restaurant and associated garden (laid 150 years ago as a city park) have become one of the cultural hotspots of North Amsterdam. Paradiso holds concerts at **Tolhuistuin,** and in the summer there's a program of live music, DJs, and theater in the garden every weekend. Even if there is no event going on, it's a fine location with the café-restaurant, a large roof terrace, and the mysterious atmosphere of the garden. The Tolhuistour is recommended, which is an audio tour obtained at the nearby EYE or via an app. Download the free Tales&Tours app and then select the Tolhuistour for €2.69.
Tolhuisweg 5, www.tolhuistuin.nl, tel. 020-7604820, garden open Thur-Sun noon-10pm, see website for program and other opening times, Ferry 901, 907 Buiksloterweg

35 Unfortunately it's open only one weekend a month, but that's partly what makes it so special and well worth a visit. With 750 stalls, the flea market in the **IJ-hallen** is one of the largest in Europe. Thanks to the market's growing popularity you'll need to search for the real bargains, but the atmosphere is always fantastic, and special items are up for grabs.
TT. Neveritaweg 15, www.ijhallen.nl, open one weekend a month Sat-Sun 9am-4:30pm, see website for calendar, entrance €5, Ferry 903, 905, 906 NDSM, Bus 35, 36 Atatürk

WITH MORE TIME

The walks in this book will take you to most of the city's main highlights. Of course, there are still a number of places worth visiting that are not included in the previous walks, and those are listed here. Note that not all of these places are easily accessible by foot from town, but all are accessible by using public transportation.

Ⓐ If you are tired of the crowded center, just hop on a bike or take the bus to the **Amsterdamse Bos.** This nature and leisure park between Amsterdam and Amstelveen is a lovely place to go for a walk or ride a bike. There are also two children's paddling pools, a goat farm, exciting climbing courses among the trees at Fun Forest Climbing Park, and canoe and paddleboat facilities on the Grote Vijver. There are a couple of famous Dutch hockey and soccer pitches at the edge of the forest. A rowing club has regular competitions, which are held on the Bosbaan. Every summer, theater performances are held outdoors at the Openluchttheater and attract large crowds—some people gather on the benches hours in advance with picnic baskets and bottles of wine, soaking up the pleasant, relaxed atmosphere.

Bosbaanweg 5, www.amsterdamsebos.nl, Visitors Center open Tue-Sun 12-5pm, free, Tram 26 Vu Medisch Centrum, Bus 62, 246 Vu Medisch Centrum

Ⓑ Apart from Blijburg, a pleasant hippie city beach, **IJburg** is virtually unknown to many Amsterdammers, which is a pity because there is lots to see and do here as far as the new area's architecture, restaurants, and cafés are concerned. IJburg consists of six islands, of which Steigereiland Zuid is the most interesting in terms of architecture—residents were allowed to design their own homes, which are clearly visible on, for example, J. O. Vaillantlaan. There are also floating homes on the Haringbuis Dijk. On Haveneiland Oost try a modern take on pancakes at Firma Koek, while Haveneiland West harbors the lovely Greek restaurant I-Grec.

Ijburglaan, Tram 26 Lumierestraat

Ⓒ Many researchers work and study in the **Science Park**'s modern buildings. These are the offices of the science faculty at the University of Amsterdam, the

Amsterdam University College, dozens of research institutes in the area, and some 120 other companies. Even if you have little to do with information technology, life sciences, advanced technology, or sustainability, this campus is worth a visit. Several of the buildings were nominated for the Golden AAP (Amsterdam Architecture Prize), including Amsterdam University College. Also take a look at the installation, *Raw Paradise*, located in the tunnel under the train station, where artificial light from hundreds of LED lights merges with the natural light from outside.

Science Park, Bus 40, 240 Science Park, Train Science Park

ⓓ On the other side of the IJmeer is the **Muiderslot.** This imposing medieval castle with a moat was built around 1285 by Count Floris V. The castle is situated about 10 miles outside of Amsterdam in the picturesque village of Muiden. Paintings and artifacts reveal more about life at Muiderslot during the Netherlands' Golden Age. The famous Dutch writer C. Hooft lived in the castle 400 years ago. The period rooms still have 17th-century furnishings. You can also wander around the castle's beautiful gardens. A visit to Muiderslot makes a great family day out with the children, who can climb the towers or go on an exciting treasure hunt.

Herengracht 1, Muiden, www.muiderslot.nl, open Apr 1-Oct 31 Mon-Fri 10am-5pm, Sat-Sun noon-5pm Nov 1-Mar 31 Sat-Sun noon-5pm, entrance €13.50, Bus 327 From Amstel Station

Ⓔ **Broek in Waterland** is a stone's throw from Amsterdam. This village of wooden Dutch houses is surrounded by meadows and dykes. For much of its history it was a thriving village, but during one harsh period the colorful houses were all painted shades of gray. This area has large pieces of land that are accessible only by water, so it's nice to rent a boat at the edge of Broek in Waterland and take yourself on a boat trip past the dykes and through the lakes. The *fluisterboten* ("whisper boats") have silent electric motors, so you can fully enjoy the natural environment—and if you're lucky, you might be able to spot some of the many birds native to this area.

Drs J. Van Disweg 4, Broek in Waterland, www.fluisterbootvaren.nl, 3-hour rental for 5 people €50, Bus 316 from Amsterdam Centraal or get there by bicycle

Ⓕ For a long time, the polder region on the outskirts of Amsterdam between West and Halfweg was a run-down, undefined area. Then, a couple of creative, enterprising folks fell in love with this piece of nature, and now there is a lot to see and do in the **Tuinen van West.** It's a unique place where you can walk, pick fruit, ride a horse, or go for a bike ride. You'll also find **Het Rijk van de Keizer** here, hidden among the greenery. Plop down on soft cushions and enjoy an organic lunch. The venture began in the Jordaan where founder John Hannema organized evenings with theater and food. But the venue soon became too small, and John picked a perfect location in the heart of Amsterdam's pasturelands. Here you really feel that you can get away from it all, in a lovely, relaxed atmosphere.

Joris and Den Berghweg 101-111, www.hetrijkvandekeizer.nl & www.tuinenvanwest. info, open Wed-Sun 11am-7pm, Bus 21 from Amsterdam Central or get there by bike

Ⓖ **Ruigoord** lies in the heart of Amsterdam's port and has a long history. At the beginning of the 1970s, the village had 200 inhabitants and was in danger of being swallowed by the port. The local priest and a couple of village inhabitants opposed the plans and were supported by a group of Amsterdam artists. At the end of July 1973, the priest handed the artists the keys to the church with the hope they would save the village. From that day on, Ruigoord was a cultural haven with a hippie feel, where many illicit substances were taken. It became known for its anything-goes atmosphere. Although initially Ruigoord was supposed to be demolished as part of the expansion plans for the port, in 2000 it was decided that part of the village could remain. No one lives there anymore, but there are numerous galleries and studios where alternative and cultural activities are organized, and every summer sees the annual festival Landjuweel.

Ruigoord 76, Amsterdam, www.ruigoord.nl, Bus 82 from Amsterdam Centraal or get there by bike

Ⓗ If you take the ferry from behind Centraal Station to the other side of the IJ and keep walking straight ahead down Buiksloterweg, you will come to **Van der Pekstraat.** What was once a slum is now a bustling street with all sorts of interesting shops. The Pekmarkt happens on Wednesdays, Fridays, and Saturdays. Every Saturday, there's an open street podium where anyone who feels like it can perform in front of an audience. The result is often-surprising moments and lots of fun. You can buy lovely home textiles at Club Geluk, or head to Fashion & Tea for trendy clothing or a cup of tea in a cozy inner garden. You can also eat your heart out on Van der Pekstraat. Try Soepboer for the most delicious soup, Café Modern/Jaques Jour for culinary highlights, and Semifredo on weekends for an elaborate lunch.

Van Der Pekstraat, www.pekmarkt.nl, Ferry 901, 907 Buiksloterweg

Ⓘ The Netherlands, as you've seen on the postcards, features picturesque little houses, windmills, and meadows. That's the **Zaanse Schans.** This area of the Zaan waterway was set up to protect historic heritage, dating from the 18th and 19th centuries. The wooden mills, barns, and houses in typical Zaans wooden architecture were transported here from 1961 onward. Traditional crafts are still practiced in the mills and barns. There's a clog maker, a cheese farmer, and a distillery where you can taste liqueur. The area

has an interesting history rich in crafts and craftsmanship, which you can learn more about at the Zaans museum and the Verkadepaviljoen. The Verkadefabriek has stood on the banks of the Zaan for more than a century. Originally a bread and biscuit factory, over the course of its long history, Verkade produced 48 varieties of cookies and many types of chocolate, sweets, biscuits, and even tea-light candles. The Verkade family always kept a careful record of the business's development, and the result is an extensive collection of 9,000 photos, 1,000 posters and advertisements, the packaging for 2,000 items, and working machines. The collection gained a permanent home in 2009 when the Verkadepaviljoen was opened. The area is an important attraction not only for tourists from overseas, but also for locals. Mondays and Tuesdays are quieter days to visit the Zaanse Schans, or head there in the afternoon.

Schansend 7, Zaandam, www.dezaanseschans.nl, Bus 391 from Amsterdam Centraal

NIGHTLIFE

There are all sorts of ways to enjoy Amsterdam's nightlife. The main nightlife attractions are situated around the Leidseplein, the Rembrandtplein, and the Red Light District, which is also where you'll find most of the tourists. But you can still find some more mainstream clubs such as **Paradiso** and **Melkweg**, which both have good concerts.

Perhaps you prefer something more underground? Alternative options are scattered across the city in Noord on the NDSM wharf, in West on Hugo de Grootplein, or in the Westerpark. If you're looking for a drink, head for the Jordaan's cozy pubs. For same-day theater performances, look for the Last Minute Ticket Shop on the Leidseplein, and there's a good chance you'll find a half-price ticket!

HOTELS

A good bed, a tasty breakfast, and a nice interior—these are all ingredients for a pleasant hotel stay. Even more important, however, might be location. A hotel is really only good if you can walk out of the lobby and straight into the bustling city. Staying the night in the center of Amsterdam is often very pricey. Fortunately, there are a few hostels in the Center for an affordable overnight stay. There are plenty of nice areas around the Center where you can stay for a reasonable price, such Bos en Lommer, Oud-West, or De Pijp. The Center is always accessible with public transportation, but renting a bicycle makes it even easier to get around. Going out for breakfast is also no problem—there are loads of nice breakfast and coffee places around the Center. If you'd prefer a quieter start to the day, try Noord or the Eilanden.

INDEX

✳ INDEX

MOON
AMSTERDAM WALKS
SECOND EDITION

AVALON TRAVEL
Hachette Book Group
1700 Fourth Street
Berkeley, CA 94710, USA
www.moon.com

ISBN 978-1-64049-775-7
Concept & Original Publication
"time to momo Amsterdam"
© 2019 by mo'media.
All rights reserved.

time to momo

MO' MEDIA
Text and Walks
Femke Dam

Translation
Cindi Heller

Design
Studio 100% &
Oranje Vormgevers

Photography
David in den Bosch,
Evelien Vehof, Saskia van Rijn,
Tijn Kramer, Judith Zebeda,
Hans Zeegers

Project Editor
Sophie Kreuze

AVALON TRAVEL
Project Editor
Lori Hobkirk

Typesetting
Cynthia Young

Copy Editor
Beth Fraser

Proofreader
Sandy Chapman

Cover Design
Faceout Studio, Jeff Miller

Printed in China by
RR Donnelley
First US printing,
December 2019

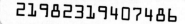

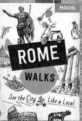